MODERN COUPLES, ANCIENT WISDOM

A BLUEPRINT TO HEAL CONFLICTS, DEEPEN INTIMACY & CREATE EMOTIONALLY THRIVING MARRIAGES

By
GANESH MANDADI

If Marriages Are Made In Heaven,
Why Live Them In silence, Pain, Or Conflict?

Clever Fox® PUBLISHING
Chennai • Bangalore

CLEVER FOX PUBLISHING
Chennai, India

Published by CLEVER FOX PUBLISHING 2025

ISBN: 978-93-6707-894-5

Dedication

To my soulmate, Srilatha, whose love, patience, and partnership have been the heartbeat of this journey.

To my family, who stood beside me in every season with faith and warmth.

And at a deeper level, to every relationship — personal and professional — that has shaped, challenged, and refined me into who I am today.

This book is as much yours as it is mine.

CONTENTS

Author's Note .... *v*

Introduction .... *vii*

1. The New Age Marriage – What's Changed? 1
2. The Emotional Blueprint – Understanding Each Other & the Inner World You Share 9
3. Healing the Inner Child, Personal Trauma in a Shared Space 26
4. The Communication Cure, From Misunderstood to Understood 37
5. The Ego Trap, Control, Comparison & Power Struggles 45
6. The Sacred Rift, When Spiritual Paths Diverge 55
7. When Trust Breaks – Navigating Infidelity & Emotional Affairs 68
8. Intimacy & the Invisible Gap, Reigniting Emotional and Physical Closeness 79
9. The Family Web, In-laws, Boundaries & Identity Loss 90

10. Parenting on the Same Page, Raising Children Without Losing Each Other 101
11. When Careers Collide, Balancing Ambition, Growth & Togetherness 115
12. The Finance & Freedom Balance, Money, Trust & Partnership in Marriage 128
13. Purposeful Partnership, Designing a Marriage That Serves the World 141
14. The Ritual of Renewal, Sustaining Love with Sacred Practice 157

Conclusion: From Conflict To Connection, From Love To Legacy.. 166

Bonus Resource Page... 172

About the Author – Ganesh Mandadi 178

AUTHOR'S NOTE

In a world that's more connected than ever before, our hearts often feel lonelier than ever. As I journeyed through my own life, across boardrooms, farms, success, failure, speaking gigs, coaching, and fulfillment, one truth became strikingly clear: *no success is meaningful if our relationships are silently suffering.*

Modern Couples, Ancient Wisdom is not just a book. It's a heartfelt offering, a bridge between timeless spiritual truths and today's emotional challenges. A gentle hand for couples walking through the fog of disconnection, trying to remember why they fell in love in the first place.

Our generation is racing ahead, building businesses, chasing goals, and managing constant noise. But in this rush, we're forgetting the sacred pause. The rituals. The healing conversations. The shared vision that turns two people into a *soul-aligned partnership*.

This book is born out of lived experience, my own 47-year life journey, 22 years of marriage with my wife, and the many couples I've had the privilege to interview and coach. It doesn't promise perfection. But it offers *practical blueprints, ancient insights, and soulful tools* to help you feel seen, heard, and held again in your relationship.

If even one couple reads this and says, *"We finally started listening again. We finally started loving consciously again,"* then this book has served its purpose.

Thank you for giving this book a place in your life. My sincere hope is that it inspires you not just to stay together, but to *thrive together, emotionally, spiritually, and soulfully*.

With warmth and gratitude

Ganesh Mandadi

Author | TEDx & Josh Talks Speaker | SoulSync Relationships™ Founder

INTRODUCTION

"Surgery is the last resort when medication fails; similarly, divorce should be the final option when all healing tools in a relationship have been truly tried."

– **Ganesh Mandadi**

I didn't write this book just as a relationship and life balance coach.

I wrote it as a *husband*, a *father*, and a *man* who has walked the winding, often messy, yet deeply meaningful road of love for over two decades, *not in theory, but in real life*.

My wife and I have been together for over 22 years, a journey that began with *three years of friendship*, blossomed into a *love-cum-arranged marriage*, and evolved into *nineteen years of shared life*, filled with parenting, purpose, celebration, and challenges. Together, we've raised two incredible children, our daughter *Harshitha* and our son *Shivansh*, and built a life that wasn't always easy, but was always honest.

We've weathered emotional storms and navigated seasons of financial uncertainty. We've laughed through the mundane, cried through the misunderstandings, and stood by each other when the world around us felt uncertain and overwhelming. *We didn't just stay married, we kept choosing one another.* Not just on the good days when love flows effortlessly, but especially on the hard days, when *love has to be a conscious decision more than just a feeling.*

Through all of it, one truth echoed louder than anything else: *Marriage isn't a destination, it's a lifelong journey and a sacred spiritual path.*

It's a fire that refines you. A mirror that shows you both your light and your shadow. It's not about perfect compatibility or fairy-tale romance, it's about *soulful partnership*. About creating a sacred container where both people can be seen, felt, heard, and loved into their fullest selves.

Over the years, as I listened to hundreds of couples in my coaching practice, I began noticing a painful pattern:

Most marriages don't break down due to a lack of love. They break due to a lack of *emotional intimacy*, *rituals of connection*, and *intentional effort*.

In today's fast-paced world, where notifications replace real conversations and reels substitute for real emotions, we are more distracted, more drained, and more disconnected than ever before. And this disconnection isn't just digital, it's emotional, spiritual, and intimate.

Yet, within this very chaos, lies a hidden gift. A *sacred calling.* To *reclaim the ancient wisdom* of relationships, not as outdated scripts, but as timeless truths that can heal, guide, and uplift modern marriages.

This book is born from that calling.

Why This Book?

Because couples like us deserve more than survival. We deserve sacred connection, emotional safety, passionate intimacy, and purposeful partnership.

We deserve to *thrive.*

I'm not offering you a formula. I'm offering you a *blueprint*, a SoulSync Blueprint, that integrates:

- *Ancient wisdom* (from spiritual traditions that honored love as sacred)
- *Modern psychology* (grounded in emotional intelligence and neuroscience)
- *Personal reflections* (from my life as a partner and a guide)
- *Practical rituals* (that fit into our busy lives)

Whether you're in the first few months of marriage or your 30th year… whether you're in love, out of sync, or somewhere in between, this book is for you.

- If you've ever felt that your partner doesn't understand you anymore…
- If you've argued about the same things, over and over again…
- If the spark has faded and routine has taken over…
- If you're longing for emotional closeness and soulful alignment…

You're not broken. Your relationship isn't doomed. You simply need a new *language*, a new *lens*, and a new *ritual of love.*

What You'll Discover Inside

This isn't just a book, it's a mirror, a map, and a companion on your soulful journey of love, conflict, healing, and reconnection.

Each chapter is designed to touch the *real, raw, and redeeming spaces* in modern marriages, helping you pause, reflect, and realign with the relationship you truly desire.

Here's a glimpse of what awaits you in the pages ahead:

Chapter 1: The New Age Marriage – What's Changed?

Explore how modern marriages are shaped by shifting roles, fast-paced lifestyles, and digital distractions, and why traditional love stories need a new-age understanding. Explore why today's couples aren't just seeking love, they're searching for emotional safety, spiritual alignment, and deeper meaning beyond societal checkboxes.

Chapter 2: The Emotional Blueprint, Understanding Each Other & the Inner World You Share

Uncover how hidden emotional imprints from childhood and past experiences silently influence your reactions, needs, and how you connect as a couple through PIP value alignments.

Chapter 3: Healing the Inner Child, Personal Trauma in a Shared Space

Discover how unresolved childhood wounds surface in your adult relationship, creating patterns of emotional disconnection, blame, or avoidance, and learn to harmonize.

Chapter 4: The Communication Cure, From Misunderstood to Understood

Learn why couples often feel unheard even when they talk daily, and how miscommunication becomes the root of most recurring conflicts.

Chapter 5: The Ego Trap, Control, Comparison & Power Struggles

See how unspoken competition, control games, and emotional shutdowns sabotage love, and why softening, not winning, becomes the way forward.

Chapter 6: The Sacred Rift, When Spiritual Paths Diverge

Examine the deeper, often ignored layers of conflict that stem from differing values, belief systems, or life purposes, and the soul-level intimacy waiting underneath.

Chapter 7: When Trust Breaks, Navigating Infidelity & Emotional Affairs

Step into the vulnerable, painful space where betrayal lives, and understand what really breaks, and what's still possible to rebuild.

Chapter 8: Intimacy & the Invisible Gap, Reigniting Emotional and Physical Closeness

Explore the quiet erosion of closeness, where couples feel like strangers in the same room, and how that invisible distance can silently grow over time.

Chapter 9: The Family Web, In-laws, Boundaries & Identity Loss

Navigate the emotional tug-of-war between loyalty to your partner and inherited family expectations that can complicate marital harmony.

Chapter 10: Parenting on the Same Page, Raising Children Without Losing Each Other

Understand how parenting styles, emotional fatigue, and role overload can create rifts, and how staying united becomes your greatest parenting tool.

Chapter 11: When Careers Collide, Balancing Ambition, Growth & Togetherness

Delve into the challenges of professional ambition, work-life imbalance, and unequal growth journeys, and their impact on emotional availability in the relationship.

Chapter 12: The Finance & Freedom Balance, Money, Trust & Partnership in Marriage

Uncover how money conversations often carry hidden fears, power dynamics, and value clashes, and why financial transparency is emotional intimacy in disguise.

Chapter 13: Purposeful Partnership, Designing a Marriage That Serves the World

Reimagine marriage not just as a private affair but a shared mission, a sacred union that can ripple love, service, and meaning far beyond the two of you.

Chapter 14: The Ritual of Renewal, Creating Sacred Practices for Lasting Love

Learn why love isn't lost, it's often just forgotten. And how intentional rituals can turn daily routines into moments of magic, meaning, and soulful reconnection.

Each chapter is your reflection space. Your pause point. Your call to action.

✓ Root-Cause Understanding
✓ Wisdom Reframes
✓ Case Studies
✓ Spiritual Insights
✓ Couple Exercises
✓ Reflection Prompts
✓ Tools for Real-Life Practice

This book doesn't claim to fix your relationship, but it lovingly challenges you to *feel deeper, listen closer, and love more consciously.*

This isn't just a book to *read.* It's a book to *live* with your partner

My Hope for You

As you turn each page, may you feel not just seen, but *supported.* May your heart soften, your communication deepen, and your connection grow stronger. May you fall in love, not just with your partner, but with the *journey of marriage* itself.

Because real love doesn't always look like candlelight dinners and picture-perfect vacations. Sometimes, it looks like staying for one more conversation. Holding space for each other's wounds. Laughing through messy kitchens and late-night tears. Choosing each other after every misunderstanding.

Love is divine. Let's make marriage feel that way again. Let's walk together, page by page, soul by soul, to remember what marriage was always meant to be.

Let's begin.

With Gratitude,

Ganesh Mandadi
Author | TEDx & Josh Talks Speaker | SoulSync Relationships™ Founder

CHAPTER 1

THE NEW AGE MARRIAGE – WHAT'S CHANGED?

"Love is not about possession. Love is about appreciation."

– **Osho**

Marriage today is not what it was a generation ago. It's no longer just a ceremony or a social contract. It has become a living, breathing journey of self-awareness, shared vulnerability, and sacred connection. While the rituals may remain, the meaning has deepened. Couples now walk into marriage not just to build homes or raise families, but to explore inner worlds and evolve together. This chapter explores what has truly changed in the landscape of modern love, and what that means for you.

From Role-Play to Soul-Play to Explore Beyond Boundaries: A Generational Shift

My grandmother used to say, "We didn't fall in love. We grew into it." She and my grandfather shared over six decades with little more than handwritten notes and quiet evenings. Their marriage was about endurance, commitment, and fulfilling expectations. And yet, they stayed.

In generations past, marriage was largely viewed as a practical arrangement, a union forged not by emotional desire, but by familial expectations, societal norms, and cultural continuity. Love, if it emerged, was considered a pleasant by-product rather than a prerequisite. People married young, often with little emotional awareness or personal choice. They entered the partnership to build a household, raise children, uphold traditions, and fulfill responsibilities. The emotional language of marriage was often muted, buried beneath duty and endurance.

But something profound has changed.

Fast forward to today, where we have love languages, therapy, emotional intelligence, and yet, we see couples struggle to stay connected.

Have we become too fragile? Or have we become more conscious?

The answer lies not in weakness, but in awakening. Today's couples are not satisfied with survival. They crave soulful synergy. We are no longer marrying out of societal necessity. We are marrying out of a longing to be seen, felt, and understood.

This isn't a minor shift. It's a profound transformation in human relationships, from role-based responsibility to soul-based resonance. Modern couples want more than survival in marriage; they want soulful connection. They are asking:

- Can we evolve together?
- Can our love become a safe space to heal, express, and transform?
- Can our partnership be a sanctuary, not just a setup?
- Can we grow through our differences instead of growing apart?

The modern marriage is no longer a destination. It is a pilgrimage, with love as the guide and awareness as the path.

Why Do Modern Marriages Break?

> *"A relationship can be your strength or your struggle, it all blooms or breaks with how you nurture it."*
>
> – **Ganesh Mandadi**

Not because we don't care, but because we care too deeply about feeling seen, heard, and valued.

We've evolved from:

- *Enduring pain* to *expect healing*
- *Performing roles* to *pursue resonance*
- *Surviving together* to *thriving individually and as a unit*

And yet, when these deeper needs are unmet, the relationship begins to crack, not on the outside, but on the inside.

Common Breakdown Points:

- Emotional absence disguised as productivity.
- Parallel ambitions creating emotional distance.
- Gender conditioning clashing with modern values.
- Resentment from unresolved inner child wounds.
- Communication shuts down into cold silences.
- Loss of sexual and spiritual connection.

Case Study: Rishi & Kavya – Married for 8 Years

Rishi and Kavya, a real couple (names and location changed for privacy) were a dream on paper. Eight years into their marriage, they lived in an elite flat in Bangalore, managed successful careers, and parented a vibrant daughter. To the world, they were the textbook definition of "a power couple."

But on the inside, they were coexisting.

It happened on a quiet weekday night. Kavya, tired from a long workday, set dinner on the table while Rishi was lost in his smartwatch, monitoring stock trends. She waited a moment, then spoke softly:

"You track your stocks, portfolio dips faster than my emotions."

Her voice didn't rise. Her eyes didn't well up. But her sentence cut deeper than a scream.

That moment, simple, raw, piercing, shattered the illusion of "everything's fine." It forced Rishi to pause. This wasn't a marital fight. It was an emotional earthquake.

Rishi had always believed he was doing "enough." Paying bills. Being present at key family events. Taking annual vacations. But for Kavya, who lived in poetry and painted emotions with her fingers, his logistical presence meant very little.

She had been starving for presence, not physical, but emotional.

Through SoulSync coaching, a philosophy built not on perfection but intention, they began the journey back to each other. Not through grand gestures, but micro-moments of honesty.

Their Turning Points:

- *Sunday Emotional Check-Ins:* No phones. Just a diya lit, and three questions asked.
  - What felt beautiful in "us" this week?
  - What felt heavy or missing?
  - What do we want to nurture next week?
- *Evening Device-Free Time:* Every night, 8 to 9:30 PM, gadgets off. This was their window of reconnection, through cooking, music, or storytelling with their daughter.
- *Rebuilding Intimacy through Presence:* Eye-gazing, heart-sharing, and simple touch became rituals that slowly reawakened desire, without pressure.

Six months later, Kavya said, "It feels like I'm dating the man I married, only more real."

And Rishi responded, "I've built companies. But learning to sit with her silence, that's been my deepest success."

So, What's Changed in Marriage?

It's not that we love less. It's that we demand love with depth.

We've evolved:

- From *tolerating silence* to desiring emotional safety.
- From *role-bound routines* to soul-aligned rituals.

- From *managing marriages* to nurturing conscious companionship.

But when our inner needs remain unspoken, the cracks appear:

- Emotional unavailability masked by busyness.
- Modern roles clash with outdated expectations.
- Loss of playfulness, presence, and passion.

This silent erosion doesn't happen overnight. But it begins the day we stop seeing each other as evolving beings.

Awareness Before Advice: What You Can Reflect On

Ask yourself gently:

- Are we navigating life side-by-side, or soul-to-soul?
- When was the last time I asked my partner how they felt?
- Have we mistaken routine for connection?

You don't need to wait for a breakdown. You only need to begin the practice of return, to presence, to partnership, to purpose.

Closing Insight: Marriage Is a Sacred Garden

We water careers. We prune our social image. We chase self-growth. But marriage?

Too often, we expect it to sustain itself.

But love, like a garden, demands attention. It needs:

- Sunlight of presence
- Soil of honesty
- Water of consistent effort

Neglect is not cruelty. It is unconsciousness. And consciousness is the seed of all soulful change.

Reflection Practice: Journal Moment

Create a sacred pause this week. Light a candle. Sit beside your partner or alone. Reflect on these:

1. What emotional nourishment do I seek but haven't voiced?
2. What gestures make me feel seen and safe?
3. How can we return to each other this week, without fixing, but by feeling?

Make this ritual monthly. Let it become your inner compass.

Final Thought: A New Story Begins

You are not here to replay your parents' marriage. You are here to rewrite the love story for your generation. Marriage is not about staying together forever. It's about waking up together, again and again.

CHAPTER 2

THE EMOTIONAL BLUEPRINT – UNDERSTANDING EACH OTHER & THE INNER WORLD YOU SHARE

"The meeting of two personalities is like the contact of two chemical substances: if there is any reaction, both are transformed."

– **Carl Jung**

Every couple thinks their story is unique, and it is. But underneath the surface of every relationship lies something universal, an emotional blueprint quietly guiding how we connect, protect, retreat, or reach out. It's not our love that's flawed. It's our unawareness of the emotional maps we're following.

When two people come together in marriage, they don't just exchange vows; they exchange worlds. Inner worlds shaped by the laughter and wounds of childhood, by cultural beliefs, by family conditioning, and by the ways love was or wasn't expressed. And yet, most couples walk into this sacred bond with a hopeful heart, but no shared language to navigate these invisible realms.

Most of us model relationships based on what we saw growing up, not necessarily what we needed.

Ask yourself honestly:

- Did I see my caregivers resolve conflicts with compassion?
- Was I allowed to express sadness or fear without being judged?
- Did my home feel emotionally safe, or was love conditional?

Whether we realize it or not, we carry these invisible imprints into our adult partnerships.

Like hidden instruction manuals, our emotional blueprints dictate:

- How we handle conflict
- How we express (or suppress) love
- How we react when emotionally hurt or misunderstood

When these blueprints clash, *conflict is inevitable.*

This chapter invites you to open your emotional eyes, not just your logical mind. To discover the silent forces shaping your reactions, your longings, and your love patterns. Because lasting love isn't built by accident, it's nurtured by emotional fluency.

Essence of PIP's (Pre-Installed Psychological Patterns) Value Alignments Between Couples

---

> *"We do not see things as they are, we see them as we are.*
>
> – **Anaïs Nin**

Before love becomes language, before a couple speaks a single word, something deeper is already at play, the silent architecture of the inner world. Every person who enters a relationship does so with an invisible map, carved not by choice but by childhood, culture, and life experience. These are our PIP values, Pre-Installed Psychological Patterns, the emotional software we run without realizing.

In Indian marriages, where families, traditions, and social expectations often shape the couple dynamic as much as love does, understanding these PIP values is not optional; it's essential. A relationship doesn't stumble over big differences alone; it falters when these deep-seated emotional blueprints remain unconscious and unaligned.

And yet, when two people learn to gently unpack and respect these preconditions, something powerful happens: arguments soften, misunderstandings give way to meaning, and love finally finds fertile ground to grow.

What Are PIP Values, Really?

PIP values are the deep-rooted emotional responses, beliefs, and behavioral instincts formed long before your first date. They are shaped by your childhood caregivers, cultural codes, spiritual leanings, schooling, media exposure, and personal traumas. Most people don't know they operate from them, until conflict surfaces.

One partner may believe raising one's voice shows passion; the other may experience it as disrespect. One may see financial savings as security; the other sees it as emotional withholding. Neither is wrong. But their PIP values are misaligned.

It's not about changing each other, but understanding what drives each other.

When partners become conscious of these layers, they create a shared emotional language. It's like tuning two instruments in harmony. Even if their melodies differ, the song becomes whole.

Case Study: Veena & Karthik, From Trigger Wars to Emotional Fluency

Veena, a 34-year-old school administrator from Bengaluru, grew up in a conservative Tamil Brahmin household where discipline equaled love, and emotional expressions were kept tightly folded behind duty. Karthik, a 37-year-old software architect from Hyderabad, was raised in a joint family steeped in spontaneity, debate, and vibrant affection.

At first, their differences intrigued them. Veena found Karthik's expressive nature refreshing; Karthik admired Veena's thoughtful calm. But within two years of marriage, these very qualities became sources of friction. Karthik would vent his frustrations openly after work, needing a safe space to be heard. Veena, overwhelmed by his emotional intensity, would shut down, often retreating into long silences. He saw her distance as coldness. She experienced his outbursts as an emotional invasion.

"I never knew how much I needed to be understood until I constantly felt misunderstood," Karthik once confessed during a session.

What was really at play?

Their PIP values were clashing:

- *Veena's PIP lens*: Emotional containment = strength and respect.

- *Karthik's PIP lens*: Emotional expression = love and connection.

During coaching, they explored their childhood maps. Veena realized she was unconsciously repeating her mother's quiet suffering, thinking silence would preserve peace. Karthik traced his need for verbal reassurance to being the youngest child in a loud, attention-hungry home.

Once this awareness bloomed, the healing began.

They co-created a ritual called *"Pause & Pulse"*, a nightly 10-minute window where they would check in using two questions:

1. What emotion did I carry most today?
2. How would I like to be supported right now?

At first awkward, the practice became a sacred space. Over weeks, Veena learned to voice her emotions before retreating. Karthik practiced gentler tones and timing. They even framed their shared values, *peace, curiosity, and respect*, and placed them in their bedroom.

What changed? They stopped fighting to be heard and started learning to listen.

Today, Veena and Karthik say their emotional conflicts haven't vanished, but now, they feel like teammates managing a shared inner terrain rather than opponents defending their egos.

Takeaway Insight: PIP Alignment Is a Journey, Not a Quick Fix

Understanding each other's PIP values isn't about perfection; it's about presence. It's learning that beneath every overreaction lies an old wound, beneath every silence, an unspoken belief.

When couples begin to map each other's emotional software, they don't just resolve conflicts; they rewire their connection.

In Indian marriages where unspoken expectations often outweigh spoken words, the courage to decode PIP values becomes an act of radical love.

Because once you understand your partner's unseen architecture, you no longer fight the structure; you build a sacred home within it.

SoulSync Reflection Prompt: *What emotional beliefs did I absorb from my childhood? And how are they shaping the way I love today?*

SoulSync Affirmation: "We honor the codes we were given, but we choose the language we build together."

> *"Human emotions speak louder than words, drive deeper than motivation, and bring greater contentment than wealth."*
>
> **– Ganesh Mandadi**

Case Study: A Love Lost in Translation

At first glance, Anjali and Sandeep (names changed for privacy) looked like a deeply compatible couple. Married for seven years, both in their mid-thirties, they had two children, stable careers, and a warm home in Hyderabad. But their emotional climate had become stormy.

Their arguments were frequent and often over "tiny" things:

- A forgotten anniversary dinner
- The tone of voice during a morning exchange
- Unexplained silences during weekends

When they arrived for relationship coaching, they sat apart, both arms crossed.

"We keep fighting about nonsense," Sandeep said, exasperated.

"It's not nonsense," Anjali replied. "I feel invisible in this marriage."

As we unpacked their emotional blueprints, something deeper emerged.

Anjali grew up in a household where affection was shown openly, through hugs, conversations, and care. Her parents believed in expressing love often. For her, love meant being seen, heard, and emotionally affirmed.

Sandeep, on the other hand, was raised in a quiet family where emotions were managed with silence. His father rarely said "I love you," but ensured the fridge was full and the school fees were paid. For him, love meant responsibility.

They weren't wrong. Just wired differently.

Anjali wanted to talk. Sandeep wanted to fix. Anjali craved connection. Sandeep sought peace.

They were not incompatible. They were emotionally lost in translation.

Healing Through Understanding: The Turning Point

Through our sessions, we introduced them to the concept of "*Emotional Blueprint Awareness.*"

One evening, they did a simple but profound activity: *Blueprint Swap Night*. They each shared a memory from childhood when they felt emotionally supported, and one when they felt emotionally abandoned.

Anjali spoke about a time her mother held her after a failure in school, whispering, "I still believe in you."

Sandeep shared how, after being bullied, his father simply said, "Be strong," and left the room.

For the first time, they saw each other not as difficult spouses, but as children with emotional legacies.

New Rituals, New Results

Over time, they began building new rituals:

- *Weekly Emotion Check-ins:* Every Sunday, they sat down and shared one emotion they felt strongly during the week, without judgment or fixing.
- *The 90-Second Rule:* When emotions flared, they paused for 90 seconds before responding, allowing space for reflection.
- *Love Languages Redefined:* Anjali learned to appreciate acts of service from Sandeep as his love expression. Sandeep learned to use words and touch intentionally, even when it felt unnatural.

Gradually, the storm began to settle.

Anjali smiled more. Sandeep spoke more.

Not because their personalities changed. But because their emotional fluency improved.

What Is an Emotional Blueprint?

It is the emotional DNA that shapes how we:

- Express love or withhold it
- React to conflict or avoid it
- Seek comfort or give silence
- Interpret our partner's actions
- Express vulnerability
- Meet or miss needs

These blueprints aren't wrong, they're just *unconscious.* When two different blueprints meet, without awareness, they clash.

You didn't write your blueprint. It was written for you, by childhood, culture, and early experiences. But now, you have the power to revise it.

Emotional Blueprints & Attachment Styles

Most conflicts are not about incompatibility; they're about *unawareness.* Here's how attachment styles play out in marriage:

Attachment Style	**Core Fear**	**Behaviors**
Secure	None	Communicates openly, trusts deeply
Anxious	Abandonment	Clings, seeks constant reassurance

Avoidant	Engulfment	Shuts down, avoids closeness
Disorganized	Trauma	Inconsistent, reactive

SoulSync Exercise

As a couple, explore:

- What attachment style did you develop?
- How does it affect your conflict pattern?
- How do you seek love, and how do you block it?

SoulSync Affirmation:

"I choose to see beyond my partner's reaction and witness their deeper feeling."

Say this aloud during moments of tension. Let it soften the space.

Reflections to Deepen Emotional Understanding

We often think our partner is triggering us. But sometimes, they are reflecting the parts of us still longing to be heard or healed.

Behind every outburst is an emotion. Behind every emotion is a need. Behind every need is a story.

Emotional fluency means being curious about that story, both yours and your partner's.

Ask yourself:

- When I get hurt in this relationship, what does it remind me of?
- Do I react from my present self or my past wounds?
- What emotion do I find hardest to express? Why?

Ask your partner:

- What does emotional safety mean to you?
- When do you feel most loved by me?
- What do you wish I understood about your inner world?

The 5 Core Emotional Needs in Marriage

These are the silent cravings behind most outbursts and arguments:

1. *To feel seen* – "Do you notice me?"
2. *To feel safe* – "Can I be vulnerable without judgment?"
3. *To feel significant* – "Am I your priority?"
4. *To feel soothed* – "Will you calm me when I spiral?"
5. *To feel supported* – "Are you emotionally and practically there for me?"

Ask: *"Which of these needs do I long for most? Which ones do I struggle to meet for my partner?"*

Case Study: "It's Not About the Tea Cup"

Nikhil & Aparna, married for five years.

Aparna kept feeling resentful when Nikhil worked late. Her complaint? "You never join me for tea." One evening, in tears, she said, "It's not about the tea. I just want to feel like I matter."

Together, they unpacked the blueprint:

- *Aparna's core need:* Emotional presence
- *Nikhil's blind spot:* Equating love with provision, not presence

They started a simple ritual, *15 minutes of screen-free tea time each evening*. Over time, arguments lessened, connection deepened.

Emotional needs aren't grand, they're small things done with intention.

Emotion Mapping Tools

Use the *Emotion Wheel* to recognize and name layered feelings:

- *Primary:* Anger, Fear, Sadness
- *Secondary:* Frustrated, Anxious, Lonely
- *Tertiary:* Ignored, Unsafe, Misunderstood

SoulSync Prompt: What 3 emotions do I feel most often in our marriage? Which ones do I suppress?

From Reactive to Reflective – Coaching Tools in Action

In the heat of emotional friction, most couples react with defense, blame, or withdrawal. But real healing begins not in reaction, but in reflection. These simple yet powerful tools are designed to shift your relationship from automatic patterns to conscious presence. When practiced consistently, they become anchors of empathy, understanding, and emotional growth.

Tool 1: The Pause Practice

Before reacting, pause and ask:

- What am I feeling?
- What story am I telling myself?
- What might my partner be feeling?

Tool 2: Mirror & Validate

Repeat what you heard with compassion:

"You feel ___ when I ___. That makes sense."

This builds safety more than any solution ever will.

Tool 3: Emotion Mapping Board

Set up a shared weekly board:

- Color code the emotions you experienced
- Celebrate emotional awareness as progress

SoulSync Practice: Blueprint Swap Night

- Set aside an intentional evening.
- Each partner shares childhood emotional memories, no blame, only curiosity.
- End with: *"What does emotional safety mean to you?"*

This deepens empathy and gives context to current behaviors.

SoulSync Workbook Reflection Prompts

1. What did love look like in my childhood?
2. What emotional messages did I absorb?
3. What do I need most in this relationship?
4. When do I feel safest? Least safe?
5. What is one emotion I rarely express, and why?

Write separately, then share. Listen to understand, not respond.

Reframe the Narrative

"Marriage isn't just about who you love, it's about how you love."

Upgrade the "how," and the "who" begins to feel like home again.

Closing Insight: Love Needs a Language

We don't fall out of love. We fall out of emotional practice.

Most couples don't lack affection. They lack alignment. They speak different emotional languages, expecting to be understood by default.

But understanding is never a default. It's a decision.

A decision to pause. To ask. To witness. To learn.

When two people become students of each other's emotional worlds, they create not just harmony, but healing.

Learn to read your partner's emotional blueprint, not just their words. Because beneath the noise of everyday life, there is always a feeling trying to be heard.

And when you begin to hear it, really hear it... Love returns home.

CHAPTER 3

HEALING THE INNER CHILD, PERSONAL TRAUMA IN A SHARED SPACE

"In most couple conflicts, it's not just two adults arguing, it's two wounded inner children reaching for love, safety, and validation the only way they know how."

– **Ganesh Mandadi**

Every couple brings dreams into marriage, hopes of togetherness, joy, and lasting companionship. But alongside those dreams, we unknowingly carry a hidden suitcase packed long before we met our partner. Not of clothes or souvenirs, but of childhood wounds, unmet emotional needs, and deeply ingrained survival mechanisms.

Why does a small disagreement sometimes feel like a war? Why does a missed call feel like rejection, or a casual comment feel like criticism?

Because it's not always the adult you reacting, it's the younger version of you, the one who felt unseen, unloved, or unsafe, still quietly running the emotional show behind the scenes.

This is the inner child. And until we learn to see, hear, and heal that part of ourselves, our relationships become playgrounds for unresolved pain.

A Personal Reflection from My Journey

When I first started my healing journey, I used to get disproportionately angry when my wife would withdraw during a conflict. I'd feel like I was being punished or abandoned. But over time, I realized something deeper: her silence wasn't about me. It was her coping mechanism, a script from her childhood where keeping quiet helped avoid emotional chaos.

Meanwhile, my wounded inner child, who once begged for attention and feared neglect, interpreted her silence as a threat. It was two inner children, mine and hers, arguing through our adult voices. Realizing this changed everything. Not overnight, but with intention.

Before you fell in love with your partner's laugh, touch, or presence, you were first shaped by the echo of your childhood. And so were they. The invisible fingerprints of childhood remain pressed into the soul's softest corners. We often don't marry just another adult; we marry someone else's history. Their pain, their longing, their coping.

Marriage isn't just a meeting of hearts. It's a meeting of inner children, two little beings still yearning for the love, safety, and validation they didn't fully receive. It is in the shelter of marriage that these unmet needs rise to the surface. And often, without awareness, we end up fighting battles that began long before we met each other.

At *SoulSync,* we understand that many conflicts are not truly about "now." They are about the echoes of then. To heal in a shared space, we must first recognize who is speaking during the storm: the adult... or the child within.

> *"Time can change and heal anything, even destiny and relationships."*
>
> **– Ganesh Mandadi**

Case Study: Radhika & Samir

Radhika and Samir came to me in distress. They loved each other deeply but couldn't stop cycling through the same pattern.

Whenever they fought, Samir would shut down, sometimes going silent for days. Radhika, on the other hand, would chase after him, cry, and accuse him of emotional abandonment.

Through our sessions, their history revealed the roots:

- *Samir* grew up in a home where his father's anger ruled the household. His only safe response was to withdraw. *Silence = safety.*
- *Radhika* was raised by a single mother who often stormed out after conflict. For her, *silence = abandonment.*

They weren't just reacting to each other; they were defending their younger selves. And once they recognized that, they began holding space for healing, not just resolution.

Meet the Inner Child

> *"The loudest conflicts in relationships often arise from the quietest unmet emotional needs."*
>
> – **Ganesh Mandadi**

The *inner child* is that part of you that carries your earliest emotional impressions, your need for love, safety, validation, and acceptance. When those needs are unmet, the child adapts by developing protective behaviors that often become emotional patterns in adulthood.

How the Inner Child Shows Up in Relationships:

- "I'm not lovable unless I'm perfect."
- "If I open up, I'll be hurt."
- "If I don't control everything, I'll be left behind."

Common Inner Child Wounds and Adult Manifestations:

Childhood Wound	Adult Behaviors
Abandonment	You become clingy or overly accommodating
Rejection	You create distance before anyone can push you away
Shame	You strive for perfection, hoping to finally feel "enough."
Betrayal	You grow suspicious, expecting disappointment.
Guilt	You over give, until your own needs become invisible

Trauma Responses in Marriage

Marriage is beautiful, but also intimate. And with intimacy comes exposure. We allow another person to see us closely… and that closeness can stir up emotional dust we didn't even know was there.

Trauma isn't just what happened. It's what your nervous system learned to do to feel safe.

We're often on autopilot, reacting from scripts written in childhood, unless we choose to heal consciously.

> *"A man who fears suffering is already suffering from what he fears."*
>
> – **Montaigne**

Case Study: The Mask of Adulthood, the Voice of a Child

Take Priya and Arjun, for example (names changed to respect privacy). On the outside, they were the definition of a power couple. Priya, a clinical psychologist. Arjun, a senior marketing head at a leading media firm. Married for four years, they appeared harmonious, yet their private life was slowly collapsing under the weight of emotional volatility.

Their sessions began with seemingly simple complaints: "He never listens when I speak," said Priya. "She overreacts to the smallest things," said Arjun. But like most surface-level disagreements, the deeper work lay underneath.

In one session, Priya broke down. "When Arjun walks away in the middle of an argument, I feel like I'm invisible again. Like I was to my father, who chose his office over me every single time."

Arjun sat still. Something had clicked. "You know," he said quietly, "Every time you raise your voice, I shrink inside. My mother used to shout just before hitting us. I guess I'm still ducking, even when there's no blow coming."

In that moment, the real marriage began. Not between titles and achievements, but between two children, Priya and Arjun, finally being seen, not as wounded or weak, but as real and deserving of healing.

SoulSync Inner Child Trigger Worksheet

Use this tool to recognize patterns rooted in your past:

Trigger Situation	Emotion Felt	Childhood Origin	Coping Response
Partner ignores texts	Anxiety	Felt ignored as a child	Over-communicate, panic
Partner critiques a decision	Shame	Criticized often	Shut down, defend

Partner flirts jokingly	Jealousy	Witnessed infidelity	Accuse, control

Use this awareness not for blame, but for compassion.

Dialogues That Heal

Next time you're emotionally triggered, pause and ask:

"Which part of me feels hurt right now?

Is this my adult self, or my inner child?"

Then gently offer words of compassion like:

Old Thought	**Inner Child Healing Reframe**
"I'm overreacting."	"I'm responding from pain. That pain deserves gentleness."
"Why can't I let go?"	"My younger self still feels unsafe. I'll offer safety now."
"They'll leave me."	"I am not that child anymore. I have choice, safety, and love."

This is what we call in SoulSync: *Reparenting through Awareness.*

Inner Child Reparenting Ritual

Mirror Exercise (Daily Practice)

Stand before a mirror. Gaze softly into your own eyes and say:

"Hey *[Your Name]*, I see you. I hear you.

You're safe with me now. You're no longer alone."

Do this for a minute. Every day. You may cry. You may smile. But you will heal.

Couple Practice: SoulSync Inner Child Share Circle

Pick a quiet evening and take turns answering these questions:

Prompt	Partner 1	Partner 2
A childhood moment that shaped my idea of love was…		
When I feel ignored, I often…		
Something I wish I had heard as a child is…		
What you can do to soothe me when I'm triggered is…		

End with a hug. Don't interrupt. Don't fix. Just hold space.

You're not healing for perfection. You're healing for connection.

Guided Visualization: The Playground Reunion

Close your eyes. Breathe deeply.

Imagine your younger self, alone on a playground swing. You, as an adult, walk up gently and sit beside them.

Now say:

"You don't need to protect yourself anymore.

You are safe, loved, and seen."

Then invite your partner into the scene. Sit together. Let the three of you, your adult self, your inner child, and your partner, form a circle of safety and presence.

This imagery often brings powerful emotional release. You can even journal what came up.

Journal Prompts: Inner Child Healing

Take time to write freely on:

1. What situation in my relationship often stirs up big reactions?
2. When I feel hurt, what do I believe about myself in that moment?
3. Can I remember a childhood moment that mirrors this feeling?
4. What would I say to that younger version of me today?
5. How can I invite my partner into this healing process?

SoulSync Closure Reflection

"Two wounded inner children cannot build a sanctuary. But two conscious adults, who honor each other's pain and offer gentle presence, can rewrite generations."

You're not alone in this journey. Every couple has pain beneath their patterns. But healing is possible, not just individually, but together.

To create a love that lasts, we must learn to hold not only our partner's hand but also their history. Their tender parts. Their wounded parts.

Healing is not about fixing each other. It's about becoming gentle enough to meet each other where the pain lives.

CHAPTER 4

THE COMMUNICATION CURE, FROM MISUNDERSTOOD TO UNDERSTOOD

"The biggest communication problem is we do not listen to understand. We listen to reply."

– Stephen R. Covey

There are moments in a marriage when a gentle touch says more than a thousand words. But there are also moments when even touch feels distant, like a language forgotten. This chapter explores a truth often whispered in discomfort but rarely examined in depth: physical intimacy is not just about bodies meeting, but about souls recognizing each other in silence, trust, and tenderness.

As couples journey through the rhythms of everyday life, intimacy can begin to feel like a ritual of obligation, not sacredness. What once felt electric becomes mechanical.

But the erosion of physical intimacy is rarely about physicality alone. It's an emotional echo. An energetic language. A response to unseen stories beneath the surface.

SoulSync views intimacy as more than closeness; it is attunement. A couple's ability to be fully present, emotionally safe, and spiritually connected determines the quality of their physical union.

Modern marriages are full of talk but starving for connection. In the rush of deadlines, devices, and emotional debris, couples often speak from reaction, not reflection.

Instead of becoming mirrors for each other's emotional world, they fall into predictable traps:

- *The Fixer*: Jumps in to solve without truly listening.
- *The Withdrawer:* Shuts down when conflict surfaces.
- *The Exploder:* Responds with intense emotions, often overwhelming the partner.
- *The Resentful Historian:* Pulls past hurts into present moments, blurring the now with then.

> *"Emotions can be felt, but the silent whispers or unsaid words in your heart can't be truly decoded — not even by your life partner"*
>
> – **SoulSync Relationships**

Case Study: Behind Closed Doors: Rishi & Kavya

Rishi and Kavya had been married for nine years. On paper, their lives were full, successful careers, two healthy children, and a beautiful home. But in their private world, the spark had dimmed.

Kavya first brought up the issue during our couple's session. "We haven't made love in over three months," she confessed, her voice trembling. "And when we do, it feels like he's just checking a box. I miss the connection. I feel... alone."

Rishi looked down, ashamed. "I don't know what happened. I love her. But lately, I feel numb. Like I'm failing everywhere."

As we traced their journey, it became clear that their intimacy wasn't suffering from a desire deficiency. It was an emotional disconnection. Rishi had been overwhelmed at work, silently carrying anxiety about finances. Kavya, feeling neglected, began pulling away emotionally.

Their once-shared sanctuary had become a silent battlefield of unspoken fears.

In therapy, we introduced "*Emotion Before Expression*", a practice where, before any physical closeness, they took 10 minutes to simply hold each other and share one emotion they were feeling. Sometimes it was "tired," other times, "grateful," and often, "vulnerable."

Over weeks, this built safety. Kavya began feeling emotionally held. Rishi began feeling seen beyond performance. The intimacy slowly returned, not because they "tried harder," but because they softened into emotional closeness.

Their healing takeaway? Physical intimacy follows emotional safety. Without it, bodies may meet, but hearts won't.

"Emotional maturity is the real graduation."

– Ganesh Mandadi

Case Study: Another Kind of Silence - Aarti & Neel

Aarti and Neel were newlyweds. The first year had been blissful, but after moving in with Neel's extended family, things shifted. Aarti felt watched, judged, and emotionally guarded.

"I love him," she said during a session. "But I feel like I have to hide my affection. Like I can't fully be a wife in this house."

Neel nodded, visibly torn. "I want to protect her. But if I push back against my family, it creates tension. So I just keep quiet."

Their physical intimacy had reduced drastically, leading to more misunderstandings.

With guided support, Neel began setting gentle boundaries with his family. Aarti, with Neel's support, created a private space in the house that was solely theirs, a corner of intimacy and privacy.

Together, they also practiced the "Heart Mapping Exercise", where once a week, they sat down and shared:

- One thing they appreciated about the other.
- One moment in the week, they felt emotionally connected.
- One area they wished to deepen intimacy.

Over time, that emotional nourishment created safety. The room they had physically withdrawn from now held warmth again. Their takeaway? Intimacy thrives where love feels safe to land.

*E*motional safety is not a luxury in marriage; it's the foundation. Communication becomes healing when:

- You're allowed to speak your truth without punishment.
- You're heard with presence, not judgment.

- You feel validated even if your partner sees things differently.

Tools for Conscious Communication

> *"Silence isn't always strength — at times, it steals your peace."*
>
> – **Ganesh Mandadi**

To help couples shift from misunderstanding to *meaningful connection*, we use proven tools that blend science with soul.

1. The Feelings Wheel

Most couples only name 3–4 emotions (angry, sad, happy, fine). The *Feelings Wheel* expands emotional vocabulary so partners can articulate what's *underneath* the reaction. Is it guilt? Shame? Disappointment? Longing?

Insight: Naming an emotion is the first step to taming it.

2. The 5-Minute Daily Check-In

A small ritual with big impact. Spend 5 intentional minutes a day asking:

- What's one thing that went well today?
- What's something on your mind?
- How can I support you better?

Practice Tip: This isn't a time to fix, it's a time to *witness.*

3. Intentional Dialogue (Imago Therapy Inspired)

This structured method rewires conflict into connection.

Mirror: "What I hear you saying is…"

Validate: "That makes sense because…"

Empathize: "I imagine you might be feeling…"

Coaching Insight: Couples who use mirroring techniques build emotional trust *7x faster*. Why? Because feeling understood dissolves defensiveness.

Workbook Reflection: "The Last Fight We Had…"

Use this powerful self-awareness prompt to break the autopilot cycle.

1. What triggered me the most?
2. What emotion was beneath my reaction?
3. What need did I fail to express?
4. What could I say differently now?

Journaling Prompts for Deeper Intimacy:

1. When did I last feel fully connected with my partner?
2. What helps me feel emotionally safe in physical closeness?
3. What fears or assumptions do I carry about intimacy?

4. What would I like to receive more of in our intimate life?
5. What am I afraid to ask for?

Healing happens when vulnerability replaces accusation.

SoulSync Affirmations for Heartfelt Communication

- "I choose words that heal, not harm."
- "My partner is not my opponent. Our conflict is our classroom."
- "I listen not to reply, but to understand."
- "Every difficult conversation is an invitation to grow together."

Closing Thought

Communication isn't about polished words or perfect timing; it's about being *present* with each other, even when it's messy. In today's distracted world, the act of *deep listening* and *honest expression* is not just rare, it's *revolutionary.*

At SoulSync Relationships™, we've seen transformations not because people learned new words, but because they embraced new *ways of being*, open, honest, and attuned.

CHAPTER 5

THE EGO TRAP, CONTROL, COMPARISON & POWER STRUGGLES

"When ego goes out the door, love walks in. Relationships don't thrive on who wins; they thrive on who softens first."

– SoulSync Relationships

Marriage often starts with sweet surrender, the way two souls willingly lean into one another, choosing presence over pride, connection over control. But with time, something shifts. Subtle yet potent, the ego begins to creep in. It doesn't bang on the doors; it whispers through reactions. A raised brow here, a defensive silence there. Suddenly, the sacred bond feels like a battlefield, with no declared war, just unspoken rivalries.

What many couples don't realize is that the ego doesn't always shout. Often, it simply outsmarts. It makes us believe we're protecting ourselves when, in truth, we're protecting our wounds. At SoulSync, we gently guide couples to not destroy their ego, but to dance with it, with awareness and compassion. The goal isn't to win, but to witness.

The Silent Hijacker, Ego in Marriage

Ego seeks separation; love seeks unity. Both often wear similar masks until you learn to see clearly, not with your eyes, but with your heart. In most relationships, ego doesn't announce itself loudly. It tiptoes in, disguised as righteousness, masked in comparisons, or concealed behind emotional withdrawals. It says things like:

"I deserve more appreciation."

"Why did they get the credit?"

"I'm right. They just don't get it."

As a relationship coach, I've witnessed how ego quietly turns soulmates into silent rivals. What begins as subtle irritation snowballs into an emotional cold war, where power replaces presence, validation outweighs vulnerability, and the relationship becomes a tug-of-war rather than a graceful dance of togetherness.

> *"In any relationship, the respect and love you receive will never exceed what you give to others."*
>
> **– Ganesh Mandadi**

Case Study: The Invisible Saboteur, How Ego Wears a Mask

Take the story of Rhea and Karthik (names changed), a couple who reached out during a particularly rough patch in their 10-year marriage. Rhea felt unappreciated, often complaining that Karthik never acknowledged her emotional labor. Karthik, on the other hand, felt invalidated, as if nothing he did was ever good enough.

Their conflicts were never explosive. Instead, they were laced with sarcasm, comparison, and withdrawal. Rhea would say, "Other husbands at least plan date nights," and Karthik would quietly respond, "Try being grateful once in a while."

In a session, Rhea revealed, "I grew up being compared to my siblings all the time. If I scored 90, my brother's 95 was what mattered. That comparison became my language."

Karthik confessed, "I was the youngest. Always told to stay quiet. So when Rhea criticizes me, I shrink. But I cover it up with indifference."

What was playing out wasn't a conflict between two adults. It was a survival of wounded selves, camouflaged by ego.

Through gentle coaching and consistent practice, they began pausing in conflict. They learned to name their emotional state before their opinion. Rhea would say, "I feel invisible right now," instead of, "You never notice me." Karthik began saying, "I'm feeling small, not because of you, but because something old is being stirred."

As soon as the ego was acknowledged, its grip loosened.

How Ego Shows Up in Relationships

Let's not villainize the ego. It's simply a protector, but when it runs unchecked, it builds walls instead of bridges. In SoulSync coaching, we recognize three dominant ego patterns:

1. *Control:* One partner decides what's best, from parenting styles to dinner menus.
   Rooted in: Fear of vulnerability or unresolved anxiety.
   Example: Rhea always insisted on how their son should study, invalidating her partner's methods. Beneath that control was her academic trauma, a fear of "not doing enough."
2. *Comparison:* Partners measure each other against friends, parents, or even societal standards.

Rooted in: Self-worth issues and cultural conditioning. *Example:* Kartik once told his wife, *"Even your sister juggles kids and work better than you."* It crushed her spirit. He later confessed that he was actually feeling like a failure at his job and projecting that shame outward.

3. *Power Struggles:* Each partner tries to "win" arguments, dominate conversations, or prove their emotional labor.

Rooted in: A subconscious belief that relationships are battlegrounds, not playgrounds.

Healing Shift: Winning in love isn't proving you're right, it's showing up in ways that are real.

Case Study: Tara & Aman, The Game of "Who Hurts Less"

Tara and Aman (names changed) had been married for six years when they found themselves entangled in a toxic pattern. Whenever Tara brought up emotional needs, Aman dismissed them as "drama." And whenever Aman tried to set boundaries around his time, Tara accused him of being "cold."

The deeper story was this: Tara grew up watching her mother suppress her dreams to keep the family happy. Subconsciously, she equated love with sacrifice. Aman, on the other hand, was raised in a household where vulnerability was weakness. He learned that stoicism equaled strength.

Their arguments weren't about the dishwasher or date nights. They were about being seen, heard, and valued.

In a breakthrough session, Aman shared, "When Tara asks for emotional connection, I feel like I'm being asked to do something I was never taught. And I'd rather pretend I don't care than admit I feel lost."

Tara, tearing up, whispered, "I thought needing love made me needy. Now I see, it's just human."

We introduced them to the SoulSync tool called "Emotion Before Expression." Before any difficult conversation, they first identified their core emotion. Was it fear? Shame? Insecurity? Then, only after naming it, they could speak their truth, not from ego, but from essence.

Within weeks, their conversations softened. The power games lessened. The silence turned into safe pauses. They stopped trying to win and began trying to witness.

The Spiritual Mirror, Seeing Ego Clearly

In Vedanta, ego is referred to as ***"Ahamkara"***, the "I-maker" that separates us from our true essence. At *SoulSync*, we don't aim to destroy the ego, but rather to build awareness around its patterns and gently invite it to soften.

The ego pushes us to speak from our narrative. The soul invites us to speak from our need. When couples start expressing, "I feel unseen," instead of "You never notice me," the energy shifts from blame to vulnerability.

Ego says, "Fix your tone." Soul says, "I miss our closeness."

And that single shift opens the heart.

Inner Reflection Questions:

- Every time you argue with your partner, ask yourself, Am I fighting to be heard, or fighting to be right?
- Is this argument about my partner… or about my fear of being unworthy?
- Can I allow both truths to coexist without needing to dominate?

Ego Check-In - Tools for Healing Ego Patterns

Situation	Ego Reaction	Conscious Response
Partner corrects me in public	"They make me look small."	"That felt tough. Can we discuss it in private?"

My partner earns more or less	"I feel superior/ inferior."	"We both contribute in our ways, let's align on our dreams."
Disagreeing on parenting	"Only I know what's best."	"Let's explore both our perspectives without making it a contest."

Healing Scripts to Replace Ego Traps

Ego Trap	Healing Script
"I do more than you."	"Can we pause to honor what each of us brings to the relationship?"
"You're not like my parent."	"Can we celebrate our uniqueness rather than relive old roles?"
"I'm always right."	"I have a strong opinion, but I'd love to hear your truth, too."

Couple Practice: The Power Exchange Ritual

One of the most powerful *SoulSync* couple exercises. Here's how:

1. *Sit facing each other,* in silence, for 2 minutes.
   Observe your mind. Ego hates stillness; you'll see it resisting.
2. *One partner shares* a moment they felt unseen or dominated.

The other only listens, no fixing, no rebuttal.

3. *Switch roles.*
4. *Mutual Reflection Questions:*
   - What touched me in their words?
   - Where did I want to interrupt or defend myself?
   - What ego need got triggered in me?

"Repeat weekly. Healing is in consistency, not intensity."

Ego Inventory: A Journaling Practice

Prompt	Your Response
I feel the need to control when…	
I compare myself when…	
I get triggered by…	
I crave acknowledgment most when…	
One recurring power struggle is…	

Journal Prompts for Couples

1. What does "being right" fulfill in me emotionally?
2. How does comparison show up, silently or openly, in our relationship?
3. Have we ever turned love into a scoreboard?
4. What's one small area I can surrender control and invite co-creation?

SoulSync Note: Journaling isn't just about reflection, it's about releasing what no longer serves.

Closing Reflection

A conscious relationship isn't one without ego. It's one where both partners have learned to notice ego's arrival and lovingly ask it to sit down, not take the wheel.

True love doesn't say, "I was right." It says, "I want to understand."

In the world of SoulSync, the real win is not in the argument, it's in the awareness that follows. Because when ego quiets, love finally gets a chance to speak.

And in that silence, everything begins to heal.

CHAPTER 6

THE SACRED RIFT, WHEN SPIRITUAL PATHS DIVERGE

"Spiritual differences don't break bonds; emotional distance does. Intimacy does not from divergence, but from the absence of genuine presence."

– Ganesh Mandadi

In the beginning of many relationships, spiritual connection often takes a back seat. There's romance, attraction, shared goals, and the excitement of building a life together. But as couples settle into routines and real-life challenges, a deeper layer of connection, or lack thereof, starts to surface.

That's where spiritual intimacy and value alignment come in. When left unattended, subtle differences in spiritual beliefs, moral values, or existential life views can become silent fault lines that cause recurring friction.

What many call "irreconcilable differences" are often not about religion or ritual but about the soul's yearning to be understood, respected, and accompanied on its inner journey. Spiritual misalignment doesn't shout, it whispers. And if we don't listen, those whispers turn into a silent scream, tearing intimacy from its roots.

At SoulSync, we refer to such moments not as failures but as Sacred Rifts, opportunities wrapped in discomfort. These are invitations for two souls to reflect, recalibrate, and rise.

Case Study: The Lonely Pilgrim, Aanya and Viraj

Aanya and Viraj, both in their early 30s, were successful professionals based in Bangalore. From the outside, they had it all: a lovely home, thriving careers, and a seemingly peaceful marriage. But within, Aanya carried a quiet ache.

She was a deeply spiritual woman. Her mornings began with meditation and chanting, her weekends involved retreats or reading holy scriptures, and her heart often overflowed with a longing to discuss the nature of life and purpose. Viraj, while supportive in his way, saw spirituality as something abstract, too poetic, too impractical. He believed in facts, numbers, and the tangible world.

Their conversations began fading. Aanya felt unheard, as though a core part of her was invisible. Viraj, on the other hand, began feeling pressured to "perform" spirituality, to sit in meditations he didn't believe in or accompany her to events he found meaningless. The resentment grew, cloaked in politeness.

In our SoulSync sessions, Aanya finally broke the silence: "It's not that I want him to believe what I believe. I just want him to *believe in me*, in this part of me."

That sentence became a key. Viraj realized it wasn't about rituals or religion. It was about emotional presence, honoring what mattered to his wife, even if he didn't fully resonate with it. He began asking questions out of curiosity, not compliance. He started lighting a diya with her every Friday, not as a believer, but as a witness to her light.

Healing Takeaway: Spiritual intimacy begins when we stop trying to convert and start trying to connect. You don't need shared beliefs to have shared sacredness. You need respect.

Applied Technique: Soul Window Conversations. Once a week, they sat together and asked:

- What did your soul long for this week?
- Did anything feel sacred or hollow? They didn't always understand each other's answers, but they listened. And that healed more than agreement ever could.

What Is Spiritual Intimacy?

> *"True connection goes beyond physical intimacy and material life; couples bonded emotionally and spiritually discover deeper happiness and long lasting fulfillment."*
>
> – **SoulSync Relationships**

Spiritual intimacy is often misunderstood. It's not just about shared religious practices or philosophical views. It's not about chanting together or agreeing on life after death. It's the ability to sit across from your partner and say, "I may not walk your path, but I honor your feet."

It's in the silence that one doesn't feel awkward. In holding each other's truth without turning it into a debate. In blessing one another's inner journey, even when you don't fully understand it.

Spiritual intimacy is when love stops seeking validation and starts seeking reverence. It's about *seeing* your partner as a soul, not just a spouse.

At SoulSync, we describe spiritual intimacy as soul witnessing, being present to your partner's inner experiences, with reverence and non-judgment.

Misalignments vs. Misunderstandings

Conflicts rooted in spiritual misalignment aren't always dramatic. They show up in everyday moments:

- One partner's yearning for stillness, while the other thrives on action.
- Disagreements about how to raise children, achievement versus awareness.
- Differing definitions of what makes life meaningful.

Here's a breakdown of how value and spiritual misalignments might show up in a relationship:

Theme	Common Expression	SoulSync Perspective
Religious Differences	"You don't attend festivals the way my family does."	Rituals can differ, but mutual respect must remain.
Life Purpose Conflicts	"I want to serve; you just want to earn."	Purpose needs harmonizing, not cloning.
Parenting Values	"I believe in spiritual growth; you push for achievement."	Blend inner grounding with worldly goals.

Existential Gaps	"You don't believe in anything beyond this life."	Discuss, not convince; share meaning, not dogma.

If not addressed, these can create undercurrents of resentment. But if acknowledged, they can become powerful doorways to intimacy.

The Path of Gentle Integration

You don't need to be spiritual twins. You need to be spiritual companions.

- Start with presence over preaching. Be curious, not corrective.
- Share rituals without attachment. Light a candle together before dinner. Express gratitude at the end of the day.
- Listen without needing to solve. Sometimes the sacred is simply heard, not handled.
- Revisit each other's core values every quarter. Are you growing apart, or simply growing differently?

The real enemy of spiritual intimacy isn't *difference*, it's *indifference.*

In a relationship, having different opinions, habits, or beliefs (differences) is *not* what damages the deeper connection between two people. What truly harms the spiritual closeness is *indifference*, when partners stop caring, stop listening, or stop making an effort to understand and connect.

Reflection Prompts for the Soul

1. What part of me feels spiritually unseen?
2. Have I tried to impose my beliefs rather than share them?
3. How can I honor my partner's inner path today?
4. Can we create a new ritual that blends both our worlds?

Case Study: A Clash of Callings, Suman and Aditya

Not all sacred rifts are soft. Some arrive like storms. Suman and Aditya were a couple from Hyderabad in their late 40s, married for 22 years with two grown children. Their conflict wasn't about temple visits or religious philosophy. It was about life's purpose.

Suman had recently undergone a profound spiritual awakening after a health scare. She left her corporate job to pursue community healing, began studying Ayurveda, and started volunteering at a spiritual center. She felt reborn, finally aligned with her soul's calling.

Aditya didn't share her enthusiasm. A pragmatic entrepreneur, he saw her new path as irresponsible.

"You're throwing our stability away," he said often. "You're chasing a midlife fantasy."

The deeper issue? He felt abandoned.

Suman was pouring her heart into her new life, but left little space for their marriage. Aditya began withdrawing, and resentment turned into ridicule. She accused him of being shallow; he accused her of becoming delusional. Their spiritual paths weren't just diverging; they were colliding.

In our work together, we unpacked the unspoken grief. Aditya admitted, "I'm scared. I don't know who you are anymore. I don't recognize this version of you."

Suman wept. "I'm not trying to leave you behind. I'm trying to find myself. Can we find a way to stay connected even if our roads look different?"

Healing Takeaway: Spiritual growth should not be isolated. Transformation is real, but so is togetherness. When one partner evolves, they must remember the art of invitation, not abandonment.

Applied Technique: Value Mapping. They created a shared ritual every fortnight:

- One evening to immerse in Suman's world (a healing circle, a spiritual book reading)

- One evening to remain grounded in their old shared space (a dinner date, a game night). This helped them merge the old and new, building a bridge between identities.

Nourish These Four Pillars of Spiritual Intimacy

> *"When two souls truly meet, silence becomes sacred, and differences become doorways to deeper connection."*
>
> **– SoulSync Relationships**

---

1. Presence over Preaching

Don't try to convince your partner. Instead, be present. True spiritual intimacy begins when both partners can *be* with each other in full acceptance, without reservation.

2. Ritual Sharing

Create small rituals that honor both perspectives:

- Light a candle together before dinner.
- Share one learning of the day that touched you deeply.
- Practice a moment of silence together every Sunday.

These simple acts build sacredness without forcing ideology.

3. Sacred Listening

Hold space for spiritual conversations, not debates. Listen to each other's life philosophies, dreams, or fears without jumping to "fix" or "correct." Sometimes, being heard is the greatest form of worship.

4. Values Mapping

Once every 3-6 months, revisit each other's core values:

- What's changed?
- What's remained sacred?
- What do we wish to nurture more, individually and together?

This avoids "growing apart" by ensuring you grow *with awareness.*

Simple Yet Profound: Couple Exercise

1. Sit comfortably, holding hands.
2. Each partner completes the sentence:
   - "A part of my soul that feels unseen is…"
   - "A value I deeply hold is…"
   - "What spirituality means to me today is…"
3. Just listen. Let there be silence after each share.
4. Hug. No solutions. Just union.

Tool: Sacred Conflict Resolution Map

Trigger	Surface Conflict	Underlying Sacred Need
One partner feels dismissed	"You never join my prayers."	"I need emotional presence and honor."
Differing parenting approach	"You push the kids too hard."	"Let's raise children rooted in values."
Resistance to spiritual talk	"You don't care about growth."	"I long to grow together, not alone."

SoulSync Meditation: "Beyond the Body"

A 7-minute couple visualization:

1. Close your eyes.
2. Imagine your partner as light, not their body, role, or behavior.
3. Let your light meet theirs. Merge in love.
4. Let go of all roles: parent, partner, provider
5. Whisper to yourself:

"We are not here to fix each other, but to witness the divine in one another."

"I honor your journey. I walk beside you, not ahead of you. In your truth, I find another face of the divine."

Journaling Prompts:

1. Where do I feel spiritually disconnected in our relationship?
2. What shared rituals or meanings can we create together?
3. How can I accept my partner's path without making mine superior?
4. What does "divine love" mean to me in our marriage?

SoulSync Coaching Wisdom:

"Don't aim to walk the same path. Aim to walk together, respecting each path."

Closing Thought: From Disconnect to Devotion

Spiritual disconnects in marriage are not signs of incompatibility; they're invitations. Invitations to listen deeper, honor what's sacred to your partner, and co-create a space where your souls don't just co-exist but *co-evolve.*

When physical closeness is supported by spiritual intimacy, the relationship no longer merely survives; it sanctifies.

Not all relationships are meant to align perfectly in belief. But they can align in reverence, in presence, in the courage to keep showing up for each other.

Your love doesn't need uniformity; it needs unity. Not in thought, but in spirit.

Because love, at its most sacred, is not about walking the same path, but walking in the same direction, heart in hand.

That is the true *SoulSync*.

That is modern love, lit by ancient light.

CHAPTER 7

WHEN TRUST BREAKS – NAVIGATING INFIDELITY & EMOTIONAL AFFAIRS

"The worst kind of hurt is betrayal, because it means someone was willing to hurt you just to make themselves feel better."

– Unknown

Trust is the soul of a relationship; once cracked, it ripples through every touch, word, and silence. In today's world of constant digital access and emotional distractions, betrayal isn't always physical. Sometimes, it's the slow drift of connection elsewhere, the secret emotional bond, or the hidden conversations that hurt just as deeply. This chapter explores how to face such storms, not just with judgment or blame, but with honesty, healing, and courageous choices. Because trust can be broken, but with intention, it can also be rebuilt.

Redefining Betrayal in the Modern Age

Betrayal today doesn't always wear obvious scars. It might arrive in the form of a late-night chat, a locked phone, or a growing emotional bond with someone outside the marriage. In a generation where emotional availability is often outsourced, it's time to redefine what betrayal means. It's not just crossing physical boundaries; it's breaking emotional contracts. Understanding this redefinition is the first step to real repair, not just of the relationship, but of the self.

We no longer live in an era where betrayal is defined solely by physical touch. In today's digital age, *emotional infidelity* has emerged as a silent wrecking ball in relationships.

The sharpest wounds in a relationship are often the ones that go unseen, the quiet betrayal of an emotional affair. It can look like:

- Feeling more emotionally connected to a colleague than your spouse.
- Sharing dreams, fears, or complaints with someone outside the marriage.

- Texting late at night and deleting the thread before your partner sees it.
- Using social media, adult content, or fantasy as a replacement for real emotional connection.

Stat Insight: Studies show that 45–60% of couples report at least one incident of emotional infidelity, often more painful than a physical affair due to the emotional secrecy involved.

At SoulSync, we have sat with many couples whose love didn't die with infidelity; it transformed. Some burned, some rebuilt. But in each story, betrayal was never the end. It was the crossroads.

> *"Marriage is not just about finding the right person; it's also about becoming the right person."*
>
> – **SoulSync Relationships**

Case Study: The Hidden Ache of Emotional Affairs

Ananya and Ritesh had been married for ten years. Parents to two kids, juggling work, aging parents, and a fading emotional connection. Ananya, a teacher, began reconnecting with an old college friend via social media. Their chats turned deeper. They laughed again. She felt seen.

When Ritesh discovered the chat history, his world collapsed.

"There was no sex," she pleaded. "But you gave him the version of you that I've been missing," he replied.

What followed wasn't rage, but silence. Walls built of confusion, betrayal, and wounded self-worth. In therapy, Ritesh admitted:

"I didn't feel replaced. I felt... irrelevant."

They began the SoulSync repair process, first understanding that infidelity isn't only about actions, but about energy. Who holds your secrets? Who gets your job? Who has emotional priority?

Their healing began when Ananya vulnerably said:

"It wasn't about him. It was about the part of me that felt invisible at home."

And Ritesh, through tears, responded:

"Then let's find her again. Together."

Their path wasn't linear. But it was sacred.

This speaks to a core truth: *Trust is less about fidelity and more about emotional safety.*

> *"Words lose authenticity when your tone and emotions don't match — even your loved ones won't feel or trust them."*
>
> **– Ganesh Mandadi**

The Psychology Behind Affairs

Affairs, emotional or physical, often stem from deeper relational cracks.

Common Root Causes:

- Unmet emotional or sexual needs
- Emotional disconnection or loneliness
- Escape from vulnerability or unresolved conflicts
- Seeking novelty and validation in external connections

Infidelity: The Emotional Roots:

"People don't always cheat because they want someone new. They cheat because they feel they're losing themselves in the marriage."

Modern Trap:

We live in a culture of instant gratification. When emotional needs go unmet, the mind craves dopamine elsewhere. It's easier to swipe right or slide into a DM than to sit across your partner and say, *"I feel unseen."*

The SoulSync Healing Framework

> *"Betrayal is not just about broken promises; it's about the silence that replaces intimacy and the distance that replaces presence."*
>
> **– Ganesh Mandadi**

The healing journey, as we see it, unfolds in three sacred phases:

Phase 1: Revelation and Emotional Holding

- Allow all emotions, anger, grief, rage, and numbness.
- No blame, no denial. Truth needs a voice.
- Set ground rules for *transparency* (e.g., no secret communication with a third person).

"At this stage, we don't fix. We hold space. We validate pain."

Phase 2: Ownership and Meaning-Making

Infidelity becomes a mirror, not just of what went wrong, but of what was neglected. Both partners ask:

- What did the affair emotionally represent for both?
- Where did we lose each other
- What patterns were repeated?
- Can we own our parts without shame?

True *accountability* doesn't mean shame. It means *owning the rupture with compassion.*

Example: In one SoulSync couple's circle, when a husband owned his emotional infidelity and wept for the neglect his wife had felt for years, both started seeing each other's pain as shared, not as enemies, but as survivors.

Phase 3: Rebuilding or Releasing

Every couple must answer the most honest question:

- Is there *mutual willingness* to heal?
- If yes, rebuild slowly, one micro-trust act at a time.
- If no, they part peacefully, honoring what was, without demonizing each other with grace and gratitude for the journey shared.

Case Study: When the Affair Was Physical, and the Hurt, Unbearable

Mira and Siddharth were the couple everyone admired, successful, spiritual, always smiling. But behind that picture-perfect life was a gaping void. Their physical intimacy had been absent for years, replaced by routines and polite distance.

Siddharth began an affair with a yoga student. When Mira found out, it wasn't just a storm; it was an earthquake. Her spiritual beliefs were shaken, her sense of self shattered.

At first, she blamed herself: "Did I make him feel unloved?"

Then she swung to anger: "How dare he bring this poison into our sacred bond?"

SoulSync Coaching helped them sit with their storm, without rushing to fix it. Mira explored her wound in depth. She journaled daily, cried often, and finally said in a session:

"I won't shrink myself to save this marriage. If we rebuild, it must be on truth, not convenience."

Siddharth, facing his deepest shame, didn't beg. He listened. And one day, he wrote her a letter:

"You never failed me. I failed myself. You deserved a man who chose courage over cowardice. I'm ready to become that now. Not for you. For us."

Months later, after deep inner work, they began a new kind of connection, not based on roles or repentance, but raw presence.

Their intimacy wasn't what it used to be. It was deeper.

> *"Your pain has a purpose — to make you resilient and stronger for the higher version of yourself in life."*
>
> – **Ganesh Mandadi**

Rebuilding Trust Toolbox

- *Emotional Check-Ins:* 10 minutes nightly. No phones. No distractions. "What hurt today? What healed today?"
- *Transparency Agreements:* Openness in communication. Not to control, but to rebuild safety.
- *Sacred Renewal Rituals:* Rewriting vows. Visiting places of memory. Creating new shared dreams.
- *Therapy Technique Spotlight:* The Trust Ladder

Step	Action
1. Acknowledgement	Admit the breach without excuses
2. Accountability	Take ownership of choices made
3. Transparent Behavior	No secrecy; share honestly
4. Emotional Investment	Re-learn how to emotionally show up
5. Repaired Intimacy	Begin reconnecting, slowly and spiritually

Spiritual Insight: The Energy of Fidelity

In Indian philosophy, the principle of *Satya* (truth) isn't just about words; it's about alignment. Infidelity, from a spiritual lens, is when your energy leaves your dharmic path. When your heart is elsewhere, even if your body isn't.

Love, when conscious, doesn't seek possession. It seeks presence.

SoulSync Reflection Journal

- What part of me felt abandoned before I abandoned this relationship?
- Can I hold both pain and love in the same breath?
- What would rebuilding trust feel like if I led with truth, not trauma?
- Am I choosing resentment, or requesting healing?

Write to connect. Write to forgive. Even if it's just yourself.

Closing Whisper

Not all relationships survive betrayal. But all hearts can.

Whether you choose to heal together or heal alone, the first step is the same: honesty. With yourself. With your wounds. With your desires.

You are not the mistake made against you. You are the strength rising through it.

And in that strength, new love is possible. Not a repeat. A rebirth.

This is the SoulSync way. Where broken doesn't mean beyond repair. Where hurt becomes holy. Where betrayal becomes the soil in which a new self blooms.

Whether your journey leads to soulful reconciliation or peaceful separation, the path forward begins with one truth: *You are worthy of love that honors your soul.*

May this chapter be your light through the dark tunnel of betrayal, and may you find, within or beyond the relationship, a deeper version of your Self, ready to love again, more consciously and courageously.

CHAPTER 8

INTIMACY & THE INVISIBLE GAP, REIGNITING EMOTIONAL AND PHYSICAL CLOSENESS

"Intimacy is not purely physical. It's the act of connecting with someone so deeply, you feel like you can see into their soul."

– Unknown

There comes a quiet hour in most relationships where silence becomes heavier than words, and physical nearness masks emotional distance. It's the moment when you realize your partner may be lying right next to you, but your souls feel miles apart. This drift is not sudden; it's subtle, patient, and often unnoticed until one day, someone whispers, "We're roommates, not lovers."

In my work with couples across India, from bustling metros to quiet rural corners, one recurring theme stands out: people crave intimacy, but few know how to sustain it. Intimacy, unlike attraction, is not automatic. It is grown, nourished, and protected. And when left unattended, it fades, not because love dies, but because connection is forgotten.

At SoulSync, we hold a reverent view of intimacy. We see it not merely as a physical union, but as a sacred language of emotional truth, spiritual touch, and everyday tenderness. Let us explore how to bridge this invisible gap and awaken closeness again, soulfully, gently, and with presence.

Case Study: A Marriage Without Fire, The Story of Nikhil & Meera

Nikhil and Meera had been married for twelve years. They were successful professionals, doting parents, and good human beings. But one look at them together, and it was clear, something had dimmed. The laughter had become polite. The hugs, brief. Intimacy was scheduled but soulless.

Meera confided, "He used to hold me like I was precious. Now, I feel like a task, one more item on his checklist."

Nikhil felt it too, but couldn't express it. "We're not fighting. We're not cheating. So why does it feel like we're quietly disappearing?"

In sessions, we uncovered layers:

- Meera was carrying body shame post-childbirth, silently believing she was no longer desirable.
- Nikhil, raised in a family where affection was rare, didn't know how to express desire without performance pressure.

Their path to reconnection involved:

- Practicing nightly "non-demand touch", holding hands, massaging feet, cuddling without expectations.
- Rewriting their sensual blueprint by exploring what made them feel emotionally safe and physically honored.
- Meera journaling affirmations to reclaim her body as sacred, not just functional.
- Nikhil learning to give without a goal, presence without pressure.

The result? The intimacy returned, not with fireworks, but with soft candles, slow dances in the kitchen, and conversations that felt like touch.

Their key realization: "It wasn't intimacy we were missing. It was soul-touch."

The Nature of the Intimacy Gap

Intimacy is multi-dimensional. When couples say "we've lost connection," it often points to a complex blend of disconnection:

- *Physical Intimacy* may fade.
- *Emotional Closeness* becomes transactional.
- *Spiritual Togetherness* gets buried under duties.
- *Intellectual Sharing* diminishes into logistical conversations.

And here's what most miss:

The physical gap is usually the last symptom.

The deeper wounds begin *emotionally and energetically.*

To reignite closeness, couples must first feel emotionally safe; then, physical intimacy becomes a celebration, not an obligation.

The 4 Types of Intimacy – The SoulSync Wheel

Type	Expression	SoulSync Insight
Emotional	Feeling safe to share, cry, and express	*Often the first to collapse in conflict zones*

Physical	Touch, closeness, sex, cuddles	*Needs gentle rebuilding, not quick fixes*
Intellectual	Dreaming together, debating, learning	*Creates admiration & mental bonding*
Spiritual	Praying, meditating, and being still together	*Fuels deep soulful companionship*

Common Causes of Intimacy Disconnect

Let's call out the silent culprits that quietly dissolve connection:

- *Emotional Suppression:* Bottled resentment kills desire.
- *Parenting Overload:* When "mom" and "dad" replace "lover" and "partner."
- *Digital Distractions:* Scrolling beside each other replaces soul-touching moments.
- *Body Image Insecurity:* Feeling unattractive or ashamed of how we've changed.
- *Cultural Conditioning:* Especially in Indian households, where pleasure and sensuality are taboo for women after motherhood.
- *Unhealed Traumas:* Past betrayals, abuse, or childhood wounds that make touch feel unsafe.

Case Study: The Long Wait, Kavitha & Arun's Intimacy After Infidelity

Kavitha and Arun's story was more complex. Ten years into marriage, after a long emotional winter and a brief separation, Arun confessed to a one-time affair.

The betrayal shattered Kavitha.

But after months of therapy and deep soul-searching, they both chose to rebuild. Still, intimacy, especially physical, proved to be the hardest mountain to climb.

Kavitha shared: "I want to be close to him again. But every time he touches me, my mind flashes back to *her*."

What worked?

- *Emotional Rituals Before Touch:* Arun would check in, "How does your heart feel today?", before any physical intimacy.
- *Cleansing Ceremony:* Together, they wrote down all the memories of hurt and guilt on paper, burnt them under the stars, and planted a jasmine sapling over the ashes, a symbol of regrowth.
- *Sensual Mindfulness:* They practiced silent eye-gazing, forehead touches, and breathing in sync, slowly allowing touch to become safe again.

- *Fantasy Hour with Boundaries:* Arun gave Kavitha space to express her sensual imagination, without shame or judgment.

Months later, intimacy didn't just return; it deepened. Kavitha once said, "He touches me now like he's touching my forgiveness. And I let him, because I feel whole again."

Emotional Intelligence Tools to Reignite Intimacy

Tool 1: The Intimacy Inventory Dialogue

A safe weekly ritual. Ask and answer:

- "When do I feel emotionally connected to you?"
- "What kind of touch do I crave but hesitate to ask for?"
- "What makes me feel emotionally unsafe or rejected?"

Purpose: Naming desires and fears brings them into conscious healing.

Tool 2: Touch Without Expectation Ritual

Spend *10 minutes daily* in physical closeness without sexual goals.

- Holding hands silently
- Massaging each other's feet
- Sitting forehead to forehead and breathing

Why? This rebuilds trust in physical space and removes pressure-performance cycles.

Tool 3: Sensual Mindfulness Exercise

Light a candle. Sit close. Breathe in sync.

Now, each partner says one appreciation or affirmation:

"I love how your presence makes me feel safe."

"I honor how your body has held our life together."

Impact: Restores reverence to touch.

Tool 4: Fantasy Sharing – Without Judgement

Create a playful "What if?" hour. Share:

- Sensual dreams
- Desires you've never voiced
- Curiosities you'd like to explore together

No judgment. No pressure to act. Just openness.

This ritual helps couples reclaim imagination, play, and possibility.

Reflections & Realizations

1. *SoulSync Reflection Map:* On a scale of 1–10, how intimate do I feel emotionally and physically with my partner?

2. *The Safe-Touch Ritual:* Sit silently for 5 minutes holding hands. Say one thing you appreciate about each other. No expectations, just presence.
3. *Sensual Journaling:* Each partner writes:
   - What touch feels safe to me?
   - What makes me feel unseen in our physical space?
   - What is one thing I want to explore but fear expressing?
4. *The 10-Minute Pillow Talk:* No logistics. Just answer:
   - What made me smile today?
   - What made me think of you unexpectedly?
   - What's one way I missed you this week?

Spiritual Affirmation:

"I deserve to be touched with love, seen with reverence, and desired without condition."

Vedic Insight:

In the Indian spiritual tradition, Kama (desire) is not a sin; it is one of the four Purushottam (life goals), alongside Dharma (duty), Artha (wealth), and Moksha (liberation). When desire is rooted in love and reverence, it becomes a spiritual path.

Reclaiming sensuality is not about seduction; it is about sanctity.

As Rumi said: *"With life as short as a half-taken breath, don't plant anything but love."*

"Sacred sensuality is a path of devotion, not deviation."

Coach Ganesh Mandadi's Take, Personal Note

In many couples I've coached, from high-powered executives to homemakers in rural Telangana, the theme is the same:

They don't want *more intimacy.*

They want *more presence.*

They want to feel wanted… not needed.

A woman once told me:

"He helps pay the bills. But when he touches me, I feel like he's checking a chore off a list."

And that broke my heart.

Because this is not about failure. It's about forgetting how to choose each other *daily*, emotionally, spiritually, and physically.

Key Takeaways

✓ Intimacy gaps are signals, not death sentences.
✓ Talking about sensual needs is healing, not shameful.

✓ Sensuality is sacred when rooted in respect, safety, and soul connection.

Final SoulSync Reflection

Tonight, before you go to sleep, ask:

- *"Where am I holding back my affection out of habit or hurt?"*
- *"What would happen if I touched my partner with full presence, even just once today?"*

Sometimes, the most powerful act of love is the *soft hand that lingers a little longer*, the *eyes that truly see*, and the *whisper that says, not loudly, but truly*, *'I still choose you.'*

CHAPTER 9

THE FAMILY WEB, IN-LAWS, BOUNDARIES & IDENTITY LOSS

"The bond that links your true family is not one of blood, but of respect and joy in each other's life."
– **Richard Bach**

In India, marriage has never been just a private affair. It is a community event, a social institution, and more importantly, a merger of not just two hearts, but two families, belief systems, expectations, and at times, egos.

Unlike the Western model of individual-centric unions, the Indian marriage often echoes the age-old proverb: *"Vivaham Kutumba sammelanam"*, marriage is a union of families.

This, while beautiful in intent, often becomes the very reason for deep emotional ruptures. In-laws become indirect stakeholders in decisions ranging from kitchen recipes to career choices. The age-old dilemma of *"Wife or Parents?"*, *"Who comes first?"* doesn't just affect the couple; it shakes the entire structure of emotional safety within the relationship.

At SoulSync, we often say:

"You didn't just marry a person, you married their history, their wounds, their unconscious loyalties."

When couples face conflict, they often ask, "Why does it feel like there's a third person in our marriage?"

The answer: There often is. Sometimes it's a parent. Other times, it's a belief, an unresolved trauma, or a cultural expectation sitting at your dinner table every evening.

Having coached couples across India, from tech-savvy nuclear homes to joint family households, I've seen that the real conflict is rarely the people involved. It is the lack of boundaries, the weight of inherited expectations, and the emotional confusion between loyalty and love.

SoulSync Insight:

"What we don't consciously integrate, we unconsciously inherit."

Systemic Dynamics That Shape Marriages:

- *Guilt-driven Obedience:* A partner prioritizes parents' desires over the couple's mutual needs.
- *Identity Merging:* One partner slowly morphs into their spouse's family norms, leaving their essence behind.
- *Parental Veto Power:* Parents influence major decisions, like where the couple should live, how they raise children, or even how they emotionally show up for each other.

Case Study: Smita & Rajiv, The Invisible Tug-of-War

> *Emotional attachment is the fire that keeps love warm. Detachment is the breeze that keeps it from burning out."*
>
> – **SoullSync Relationships**

Smita was a confident, self-reliant software engineer. But within a year of marrying Rajiv, she began second-guessing even the simplest decisions, what to wear, how to cook, how much to spend.

Rajiv's mother, who lived with them, commented on everything. "Add more turmeric. My son likes it that way." Or "Why are you spending so much on a saree?"

Rajiv, like many sons in traditional families, normalized it. "That's how she's always been. Don't take it personally."

But Smita did. When Smita stopped dressing the way she liked, skipped calls to her mother to avoid comparison, and silently accepted that weekends were now "family days", a part of her began to disappear. She stopped initiating intimacy, began isolating emotionally, and eventually sought therapy, not because of the mother-in-law, but because of the silence from her husband.

In couple coaching, Rajiv discovered that his passivity stemmed from a childhood belief: standing up to parents meant being disloyal. He feared being seen as a "bad son."

In therapy, Rajiv admitted his fear: "If I side with Smita, I'll hurt my mother. But if I stay silent, I lose my wife."

We introduced the practice of *Unified Language*, speaking as a team.

Instead of Smita fighting the battle alone, Rajiv began saying: "We are finding our rhythm as a couple." Not "She wants to do it differently."

This subtle shift changed the energy in the home. Smita felt seen. Rajiv felt empowered. And even the mother-in-law, after initial resistance, softened when she no longer felt "replaced," but included through respectful distance.

Key Takeaways:

- Use "we" to present couple of decisions.

- Set soft, but firm boundaries with family.
- Don't force immediate compliance, lead with consistency, not confrontation.

His breakthrough came when he realized:

"Protecting your marriage isn't betrayal, it's a conscious partnership."

Indian Marriage Truths: What Makes It So Complex?

- *Saas-Bahu Archetypes:* Pop culture has glorified conflict, the controlling mother-in-law, the "modern" daughter-in-law. These labels create expectations even before real conversations happen.
- *Parental Overreach Normalized:* "They raised you, they have a right" is a belief deeply rooted in Indian minds. This makes boundary-setting feel like betrayal.
- *Gendered Expectations:* Sons are taught obedience, daughters are taught adjustment. When reversed, it causes guilt, shame, and confusion.
- *Lack of Couple Autonomy*: Family elders often feel entitled to participate in couple decisions, finances, children, home-buying, and even intimacy indirectly.

Reframing Boundaries, Love with Edges

Boundaries are not walls; they are bridges of clarity. They're not signs of rejection, but invitations to respect.

We often tell couples during our SoulSync coaching sessions:

"Boundaries say: 'I love you and me, at the same time.'"

Types of Boundaries in In-law Dynamics:

1. *Physical Boundaries*: Who enters your space, when, and how often?
2. *Emotional Boundaries*: What conversations are reserved for just the two of you?
3. *Decision-Making Boundaries*: Who holds the final word on finances, parenting, and life choices?

Ancient Wisdom Insight:

In Ayurveda, the body's life force, *Ojas*, gets depleted with emotional intrusion. Reclaiming boundaries is not just emotional hygiene; it's energetic protection. Preserving your couple space strengthens your shared vitality.

Case Study: Torn Between Two Homes, Deepa & Ramesh's Emotional Tug-of-War

Deepa and Ramesh, a couple from Hyderabad, had been married for four years. The core conflict wasn't about love; it was about divided priorities.

Ramesh's parents expected weekly visits, regular check-ins, and unquestioned obedience, all of which Ramesh complied with out of guilt. Deepa's parents, on the other hand, were emotionally expressive and expected similar attention, which often didn't happen.

Tension escalated during festival seasons. Whose home first? Whose rituals mattered more?

Deepa once broke down, saying, "He is a son there, but here, I feel like an outsider in my marriage."

The deeper issue wasn't just logistics. It was an identity imbalance.

We implemented the *Dual Root Ritual*, an agreement that both families would be honored, but never at the cost of their emotional well-being. They created:

- A yearly festival calendar in advance.
- Equal time split during holidays.
- A sacred space in their home representing both family roots, pictures, traditions, and gratitude notes.

It wasn't perfect, but it was intentional.

Key Insight: Loyalty to one's parents should not require emotional disloyalty to one's partner.

Here are respectful ways to express boundaries:

Scenario	SoulSync Script
In-laws correcting parenting	"We respect your experience, and we'd love to find our rhythm as parents too."
Over-involvement in choices	"We value your thoughts and will decide together what feels right for us."
Frequent surprise visits	"We'd love to plan your visit so we can give you our full attention."

Tip: Use "we" more than "I"; it signals unity.

Activity: Drawing "Your Family Web"

Step 1: Create Your Personal Family Web

Draw a circle with your name at the center. Add your family, your in-laws, and even family friends. Use three different color codes to classify Conflict, Mixed Emotions, and Supportive Energy.

Step 2: Reflect and Answer

1. Who makes me feel emotionally unseen or small?
2. Who energizes or exhausts me?
3. Where do I find myself pretending to be okay?

Step 3: SoulSync Couple Sharing

- Share your webs.
- Identify 2–3 areas where you can co-create new boundaries.

Coaching Techniques: Navigating Loyalty & Identity

Remember, your role is not to fight your partner's family; it's to support your partner in healing how they relate to them.

- *The Unity Dialogue:* Sit weekly and reflect,
  - Where do we feel pulled in opposite directions?
  - What decisions are we postponing to avoid parental disappointment?
  - Avoid blaming in-laws directly. Instead, say: "When this happens, I feel…"
  - Ask your partner gently: "Do you feel torn between your parents and me?"
  - Reinforce a vision: "Let's honor them without abandoning us."
- *The Boundary Blessing:* Before setting a new boundary, say a prayer or light a lamp together. Ask for clarity, not conflict. Write down the intention and speak it with love, not defense.
- *The Family Inclusion Circle:*
  - Host a family dinner.
  - Share your vision as a couple.

- Invite their blessings, but express your autonomy.

Spiritual Practice: Releasing Ancestral Guilt

Sometimes we confuse guilt with loyalty. But real devotion is truthfully expressed, not silently endured.

Meditation Affirmation: "I can love my roots without being entangled. My sacred duty is to honor the soil and build the sky. Boundaries are my devotion to harmony."

Breathe in forgiveness.

Exhale false obligations.

Final Reflection

You did not marry to choose between people. You married to create a new center, where love flows equally, respectfully, and consciously.

Boundaries are not walls that isolate; they are gardens that protect what you're growing.

Tonight, reflect:

- Where am I confusing guilt with loyalty?
- What belief about being a "good son/daughter" am I ready to evolve?
- What does our sacred union need protection from?

And then, light a diya together. Say aloud: "We honor where we came from. But we protect where we're going, with grace, clarity, and unwavering unity."

This is the SoulSync way. Not separation. Not rebellion. But soulful integration, where no one is diminished, and the couple hood stands strong, rooted, and radiant.

By embracing the family web with wisdom, not warfare, you shift the story from survival to soulful expansion.

CHAPTER 10

PARENTING ON THE SAME PAGE, RAISING CHILDREN WITHOUT LOSING EACH OTHER

"The best inheritance a parent can give their children is a few minutes of their time each day, and a lifelong example of love."

– **O.A. Battista**

Children can bring couples closer, or quietly pull them apart. In the chaos of parenting, partners often lose sight of each other, caught in the logistics of raising little humans. But behind every successful parenting journey is a relationship that feels seen, supported, and aligned. This chapter is about turning co-parenting into conscious partnering, where love doesn't just raise children, but also holds space for each other. Because the greatest gift we give our kids isn't perfection, it's a relationship rooted in unity, empathy, and emotional safety.

The Parenting Paradox

Before the child was born, it was just the two of you. A touch, a shared meal, a glance that needed no words. But the moment a child enters a couple's life, everything shifts: sleep cycles, priorities, emotional bandwidth, and even identity. The birth of a child can feel like the blossoming of purpose, yet simultaneously, it can feel like the quiet beginning of distance between two hearts; the quiet simplicity of love often gets replaced with the noise of schedules, routines, and responsibilities.

The beauty and burden of Indian parenting is that it rarely exists in isolation. Children are raised not just by parents but by grandparents, extended relatives, and community narratives, where parenting is often a family affair involving in-laws, traditions, and unsolicited advice. The shift can be even more complex.

And amid all this, couples often forget that parenting is not a competition or a cultural performance, it's a spiritual collaboration. One that requires shared vision, conscious presence, and emotional unity.

At SoulSync, we gently remind couples: "You were a couple before you became co-parents. To raise secure children, you must first remain secure with each other."

"Marriage is the soil, parenting is the seed. If the soil isn't nurtured, the seed may sprout, but it may never thrive."

Many couples unknowingly slip into what we call the *Parenting Disconnect*:

- Children become the center, and the couple drifts to the margins.
- Unhealed childhood wounds resurface during discipline moments.
- Conflicts arise not just about *what* to do, but *how* to do it, and *why*.

We don't fall apart because we don't love our children; we fall apart because we forget to love *each other* in the process.

"Marriage is the soil, parenting is the seed. If the soil isn't nurtured, the seed may sprout, but it may never thrive."

– SoulSync Relationships

Case Study: The Disciplinarian Dad vs. The Permissive Mom

Ravi & Sneha's Story (Parents of 8-year-old Aarav and 4-year-old Isha)

Ravi, a software engineer with a military-like mindset, valued routine, obedience, and accountability. Sneha, a pre-school teacher, believed in connection before correction. She followed her intuition and prioritized emotional intelligence over structure.

Evenings became battlegrounds:

- Arguments over homework deadlines
- Tension over screentime limits
- Power struggles at bedtime routines

Each night ended not just in tired children, but in two tired, disconnected adults.

What lay beneath?

- *Ravi* felt disrespected as a father. His authority seemed invisible.
- *Sneha* felt judged as a mother. Her nurturing was seen as a weakness.

Through *SoulSync Parenting Coaching*, they rediscovered their alignment:

- Identified their *Parenting Archetypes* using our custom reflective archetype map.
- Created a *Unified Parenting Vision Statement*, a joint agreement of values and boundaries.
- Participated in a *Reflective Listening Circle* with their kids once a month.
- Committed to a *"Parents-Only Hour"* every Sunday morning, phones off, kids with grandparents, just coffee and connection.

The outcome: The children became calmer and more secure. And Ravi and Sneha? They began smiling at each other again, not just surviving, but syncing.

Core Parenting Conflicts in Modern Marriages

Many couples we coach report similar patterns. Here are the most common triggers:

Conflict Type	Example
Disciplinary Differences	One says "timeout," the other says "talk it out."
Parental Role Overload	"Why am I the only one doing the emotional labor?"
Extended Family Interference	"My mother-in-law says this is not how kids should be raised…"

Education & Lifestyle Gaps	Montessori vs. traditional schooling. Screen-time battles. Activity overload.
Projecting Past Trauma	One partner micromanages because of a chaotic childhood. The other avoids discipline due to fear of becoming their parent.
Emotional Neglect of Spouse	Attention flows only toward the child, not toward each other.

These challenges are not signs of failure. They are calls for deeper understanding, inner healing, and mutual visioning.

Case Study: The Father, The Grandfather, and the Forgotten Mother, Manoj & Rhea's Struggle for Space

Manoj and Rhea lived in Hyderabad with their four-year-old son, Ayaan, and Manoj's retired parents. Manoj was an only son, and his parents saw themselves as equal stakeholders in raising Ayaan.

From day one, Rhea found herself constantly being overruled:

- Her sleep schedule for Ayaan was dismissed as "modern nonsense."
- Homemade baby food was rejected for age-old recipes from Manoj's mother.

- When Rhea tried to introduce quiet time or gentle parenting practices, Manoj's father would scold her: "You're making him soft. A boy must be tough!"

Manoj, caught in the crossfire, chose silence. "Don't upset Dad, he means well," he'd say.

Rhea didn't feel like a mother. She felt like a tenant in her parenting journey.

It took multiple breakdowns before they came to coaching. There, the invisible triangle was addressed:

- Manoj explored his guilt-bound loyalty towards his parents.
- Rhea released suppressed resentment through emotional clearing journaling.
- A "Parenting Partnership Agreement" was created, jointly written, and read out to the grandparents. Respectfully, boundaries were expressed.

They started Sunday night check-ins, just the two of them. No parenting talk. Just love.

Today, their parenting journey isn't free of friction, but it's filled with unity. Ayaan now sees a confident mother and a confident father who stands beside her.

Their biggest win? Manoj, one day, gently told his father, "You raised me beautifully. Now, let us raise our son in our way."

Parenting Styles vs. Emotional Safety

Let's decode how each parenting style affects the marriage:

Parenting Type	Characteristics	Impact on Relationship
Authoritarian	High control, low warmth	Spouse may feel unheard; kids may rebel
Permissive	High warmth, low structure	Creates confusion; partner may feel unsupported
Neglectful	Low warmth, low involvement	Erodes emotional trust; resentment builds
Conscious Parent	Balanced presence, intentional choices	Strengthens marriage and nurtures kids holistically

SoulSync Insight: Your partner is not wrong, they're wired by different stories. *Seek understanding before you seek control.*

The Indian Context of Parenting Conflict

In Indian marriages, parenting conflicts often hide beneath layers of unspoken loyalties and generational roles. The parenting journey is shaped by not just books and workshops, but also by the advice of elders, WhatsApp messages from relatives, and school gate comparisons.

Some common Indian themes:

- *The Saas-Bahu Dynamic*: When the mother-in-law feels her experience is superior, and the daughter-in-law feels silenced.
- *The Father's Role Confusion*: Many Indian men oscillate between being providers and protectors, often missing the role of nurturer.
- *The Performance Pressure*: Kids are seen as proof of parental success, leading to comparison-based parenting.

In such a charged atmosphere, couples must build intentional alignment. Because children don't just learn from parenting. They absorb the energy of the marriage.

Case Study: When the Child Became the Battlefield, Vidya & Sharath's Emotional Tug-of-War

Vidya and Sharath had a marriage that looked perfect on the outside. Educated, urban, well-traveled, they had a six-year-old daughter, Manya, who was bright and sensitive.

But the home was divided.

Sharath believed in discipline through structure. “Children must earn their privileges,” he’d say. Vidya, shaped by a turbulent childhood, vowed never to repeat the authoritarian patterns of her past. She often overcompensated with leniency and emotional indulgence.

Bedtime arguments, conflicting instructions to Manya, and passive-aggressive remarks became the norm. One day, Manya asked, “Why do you both fight because of me? Did I do something wrong?”

That one question changed everything.

In coaching, what emerged was deeper:

- Sharath’s controlling nature stemmed from fear; his father had abandoned him as a child. The order made him feel safe.
- Vidya’s permissiveness stemmed from guilt; she feared becoming her critical mother.

Their parenting styles weren’t wrong; they were wounded.

Healing techniques included:

- Weekly “Co-Parenting Circles,” where they discussed one win and one struggle without judgment.
- A shared “Parenting Purpose Statement” kept in their room: “To raise Manya with love, honesty, and unity.”

- They practiced a Ritual of Reconciliation, holding hands after every parenting disagreement and whispering, "We're on the same team."

Today, Manya sees not just good parents, but a strong partnership.

SoulSync Tools & Techniques for Parenting Harmony

Let's move from reactive parenting to *conscious co-parenting.*

Tool 1: Parenting Love Language Discovery

Sit together and reflect:

- What did "love" look like from your parents?
- What parenting behaviors do you cherish and what do you want to change?
- What kind of parent do you fear becoming?

Purpose: This reveals hidden emotional biases, helping couples co-parent without past wounds distorting the present.

Tool 2: Joint Parenting Values Deck

Use index cards or our printable *SoulSync Values Flashcards*: Write values like:

- "We discipline with empathy, not fear."
- "We celebrate effort more than achievement."

- "We are united in front of the child."

Purpose: Brings alignment and serves as a compass during tough decisions.

Tool 3: Circle of Trust Ritual

A monthly sacred circle with the child:

1. One parent facilitates, the other listens.
2. The child answers:
    - "What I love about you both."
    - "What I wish was different."

Purpose: Builds an emotionally safe triad. The child feels heard. The couple grows as partners.

Tool 4: The 3-3-3 Check-In (Monthly)

Together, share:

- 3 things we did well as parents.
- 3 things we need to realign on.
- 3 things we'll do *just as a couple* this month.

Purpose: Protects the marriage from being consumed by the parenting identity.

SoulSync Worksheet: Conscious Parenting Reflection

Take a quiet moment to reflect and journal:

1. What are *three things* I deeply appreciate in my partner's parenting style?

2. What is *one conflict* that needs deeper understanding, not a reactive response?
3. How can we ensure that our marriage remains the *core*, not the *casualty*, of our parenting journey?

Spiritual Insight: Children as Sacred Guests

In Indian wisdom, it is believed that souls choose their parents before birth, not to be shaped, but to be supported in their soul journeys. They are not yours to shape, control, or possess. They are sent by the *Divine*, entrusted to you as sacred guests.

Let this truth ease your anxiety. You don't have to be perfect. You just have to be conscious, compassionate, and aligned.

As Khalil Gibran once wrote:

"Your children are not your children. They are the sons and daughters of Life's longing for itself... You may house their bodies, but not their souls."

Best Practices from SoulSync Coaching

- Never resolve parenting conflicts in front of the child. Agree to pause, and reconnect in private.
- Create a couple of rituals: monthly date night, gratitude journaling, or even a 5-minute bedtime debrief.

- Use emotional vocabulary with children and each other. "I feel hurt" opens hearts more than "You never help."
- Avoid martyrdom. A tired, joyless parent teaches guilt, not grace.
- Say sorry to each other in front of your child when needed. You teach humility, not weakness.
- Marriage must be nurtured during parenting, not postponed.
- Children thrive in homes where parents are emotionally safe with each other
- Conscious parenting is not about perfect control; it's about united presence.
- Your marriage is not an obstacle to parenting; it is the anchor.
- Most importantly, model what you want your child to internalize: *love, respect, partnership, and conscious choices.*

Final SoulSync Reflection

In the beautiful chaos of raising children, let's not forget: *before we were co-parents, we were partners. And before that, we were two souls who chose each other***.**

Let's parent not just to raise good children, but to *raise a relationship* where love grows deeper with every bedtime story, every diaper changed, and every disagreement healed with grace.

CHAPTER 11

WHEN CAREERS COLLIDE, BALANCING AMBITION, GROWTH & TOGETHERNESS

"Love does not consist in gazing at each other, but in looking outward together in the same direction."

– Antoine de Saint-Exupéry

We live in a world where ambition fuels purpose, and purpose shapes identity. In today's urban life, most couples are no longer split between the homemaker and the breadwinner; *they're both dreamers, doers, and seekers of impact.*

In a world where dreams demand deadlines and promotions require sacrifice, modern couples in India are rewriting the meaning of love under pressure. Gone are the days when only one partner, usually the husband, carried the career crown while the other silently supported from the background. Today, both partners come into marriage with ambitions in their briefcases and purpose in their eyes.

But ambition, if not aligned, can become ammunition.

When two dreams compete for time, validation, and space, what gets squeezed out is not work, but warmth. Shared ambition can either become the power couple's fuel or the fault line that cracks the connection. Especially in Indian marriages, where societal expectations, family obligations, and gender roles still subtly dominate, the clash isn't just about ambition. It's about identity, pride, and unspoken guilt.

At SoulSync, we often witness this silent drift. Where love is not lost, but left behind.

- Two careers can feed the bank account but starve the bond.
- Mutual ambition without emotional alignment becomes a silent battleground.
- Unspoken expectations and invisible trade-offs create invisible cracks.

What begins as a beautiful partnership of shared dreams can spiral into resentment, emotional fatigue, or a sense of isolation, even when living under the same roof.

And this isn't just a theory; it's the reality of many couples who walk into our coaching space.

> *"Success that costs your relationships or health is just another form of failure."*
>
> – **Ganesh Mandadi**

Case Study: The Promotion That Nearly Cost the Partnership, Arti & Pratik

Arti, a brilliant marketing strategist from Pune, had just received the biggest opportunity of her career: heading an international project based out of Singapore. Her husband, Pratik, a grounded civil engineer, loved his job in Pune and had no intention of moving abroad.

They had met in college, built dreams together, and always believed in equality. But when the opportunity came knocking, their fairytale paused.

"You're choosing your career over us," Pratik said quietly.

"No, I'm choosing this for *us*," Arti insisted. "This step will secure our future."

Their nights turned silent. Video calls replaced cuddles. Emotional texts became rare. Pratik began feeling like the shadow in her rising sun.

When they sought help, the real issue emerged: it wasn't just about the move. Pratik feared becoming irrelevant, to her, to society, to himself.

Together, we worked on:

- Unearthing the subconscious narratives about masculinity and success that Pratik had inherited.
- Allowing Arti to express the emotional cost of her ambition, not just the financial gain.
- Building a vision board that included timelines, emotional checkpoints, and shared rituals across distance.

They created a Sunday morning ritual, "Chai Across Borders", where they drank tea on video call and journaled together. Pratik also began exploring teaching and consulting, which gave him fresh purpose.

A year later, they were still apart geographically, but emotionally closer than ever. And when Arti returned, it wasn't to a cold house. It was to a partner who had grown, just like she had.

Their realization? Success isn't sacrifice when the journey is walked in emotional rhythm.

Case Study: Modern Marriage Dilemma: Shweta the Start-Up Visionary & Rohan the Corporate Climber

> *"Forgive others to release your emotional baggage, not because they deserve forgiveness, but because you deserve peace."*
>
> – **SoulSync Relationships**

Let me take you into the lives of *Shweta* and *Rohan*, a couple I had the privilege to coach.

Shweta, an eco-conscious entrepreneur, had just launched her sustainable living start-up. Her days were a whirl of product demos, digital campaigns, and packaging decisions.

Rohan, on the other hand, was climbing fast up the corporate ladder in a tech firm. Deadlines, boardroom presentations, and client dinners kept him constantly wired.

Their once-sweet evening rituals, dinner chats, tea breaks, and laughing over silly videos had all vanished.

Instead, their life started sounding like this:

- "My launch is more important than your meeting."
- "You never help out with the kid's homework anymore."
- "I'm tired too! Why is it always me sacrificing?"

The breaking point came not in an argument, but in a whisper from their *5-year-old*:

"Why do you both always look tired and angry?"

It was this innocent mirror that forced them to pause and seek help.

Through SoulSync Coaching, they:

✓ Created a *Joint Growth Vision Board*, both personal and couple goals.
✓ Introduced *Weekly Ambition Alignment Talks*, 30 minutes of intentional connection.
✓ Established a *Sacred No-Work Zone*, every Sunday 4–9 PM.
✓ Practiced *Emotion Check-ins*, "How are you feeling today?" instead of "What's the plan?"

The result? Their businesses didn't crash. Their relationship soared. And their child smiled more often.

"Your personal growth shapes everything — career, health, and relationships."

– Ganesh Mandadi

The Cultural Tightrope of Career Conflicts in Modern Marriages

Indian couples often navigate more than just their schedules. They juggle:

- *Family Expectations:* "Now that he earns more, why should she work?"
- *Gender Role Baggage*: The woman's success is admired publicly but questioned privately.
- *In-law Dynamics*: Working late? Traveling for work? The whispers begin.
- *Childcare Judgments*: Who's the better parent is often measured by time spent, not emotional quality.

In such contexts, couples must become each other's defenders, not silent observers.

Career-based challenges don't mean the relationship is failing; it simply means the system needs upgrading. Here are the most common friction points:

Conflict	Description
Time Scarcity	Perpetual lack of quality time or emotional space
Unequal Growth Pace	When one partner's success triggers insecurity or resentment in the other

Ego Clashes & Role Reversals	E.g., when the wife becomes the higher earner or decision-maker
Family Duty Drop-Off	Home and child responsibilities are becoming collateral damage
Poor Communication about Future Goals	Making silent sacrifices and assumptions without alignment
Career Sacrifice Syndrome	"I gave up my dream so you could live yours" syndrome

Case Study: The Startup, The Child, and the Standoff, Renu & Kabir

Renu and Kabir lived in Bengaluru. Renu had founded a parenting-tech startup that was gaining momentum. Kabir, a senior finance executive, supported her fully, in words. In reality, the load of parenting their toddler fell heavily on Renu's shoulders.

"I support your dream, but we can't ignore our child," Kabir would say.

Renu began waking at 4 AM to finish work before the child woke up. She stopped attending startup events. Her confidence slipped. Kabir, meanwhile, felt overwhelmed too, but masked it behind logic.

Their daughter, Arya, once said, "Mumma always looks tired. Papa always looks busy."

In therapy, what unfolded was profound:

- Kabir admitted he feared losing his wife's emotional intimacy to her passion.
- Renu confessed she feared being labelled a "bad mother" if she succeeded.

Their breakthroughs came through:

- The "*Role Realignment Exercise*", defines clear household and emotional duties without gender biases.
- *Emotional Journaling Exchange*: They swapped journals for a week to understand each other's inner world.
- *Sacred Sabbaths*, Two weekends a month with no gadgets, no work-talk, just playtime and presence.

Renu's startup got funding. Kabir adjusted work hours. And Arya? She began drawing pictures of a smiling mom and a present dad.

They learned that career isn't the villain. Silence is. And shared dreams don't demand perfect balance; they demand presence.

From Career Collisions to Conscious Collaboration

Here are SoulSync tools that turn ambition into alignment:

Tool 1: Weekly Career Sync Talk

Every Sunday, sit down for 30 minutes, phones off, hearts open, ask:

- What's lighting you up this week at work?
- What's been draining or triggering you?
- How can I show up better for you this week, emotionally or practically?

Tool 2: Joint Dream/Vision Mapping

Instead of competing timelines, co-create a life map. Dreams. Breaks. Children. Sabbaticals. Include.

- Individual career symbols
- Couple goals (vacations, weekend rituals, family time)
- Shared aspirations (NGO work, business ideas, creative hobbies)

This helps dissolve the "me vs. you" into "*our journey.*"

- Shared Decision-Making. Don't just inform, involve. Every major career move should be a co-created choice.

Tool 3: Emotional Availability Calendar

Block and *honor* sacred time for:

- Date nights
- Coffee walks
- Weekend retreats
- Couple meditations or journaling.

If it's on the calendar, it's a priority.

Tool 4: Weekly Appreciation Practice

Every Friday evening, take 10 minutes to share:

- "One thing I admire about how you handled your work this week."
- "One way you showed up for us, despite pressure."

Appreciation isn't a luxury; it's oxygen for relationship resilience.

Because in the end, your careers will retire. But your connection? That must endure.

Coaching Insight: If your ambition costs your partner's peace, it's not success, it's self-centeredness dressed in achievement. Recalibrate, don't retreat.

SoulSync Reflection Worksheet: Career-Connection Compass

1. On a scale of 1–10, how emotionally present are we for each other after a workday?
2. Are there any *silent resentments* or unsaid frustrations about our career dynamics?

3. Do we operate as *true allies* or as accidental adversaries in our career journeys?
4. Have we had an honest conversation about the *future we're co-building*?

Use these questions to pause, realign, and rebuild, not just your schedule, but your emotional ecosystem.

Spiritual Insight: Dharma, Karma & Togetherness

In Indian wisdom, *Dharma* is one's purpose. But the path of *Grihastha Dharma* (the householder) doesn't glorify solo success; it emphasizes *shared evolution.*

Your career is part of your soul journey. But so is your partner's. When one shines alone, the glow fades fast. When both walk hand in hand, even if the paths diverge, the light multiplies.

SoulSync Affirmation:

"We walk our purpose not in isolation, but in rhythm. May our ambitions serve our union, not suffocate it."

Key Takeaways

- Ambition should be synchronized, not sacrificed.
- Emotional alignment is the secret co-founder in any successful couple's life.

- Careers are important, but connection is irreplaceable.
- Your dream life shouldn't cost your dream partner.

Final SoulSync Reflection

Tonight, as you close your laptop or wind down from a meeting, pause. Turn to your partner and ask:

"Is our love breathing, or is it buried under to-do lists?"

Then share:

- One dream you want to chase.
- One way they've supported you this week.
- One fear you've been holding in.

Because success isn't just about what you achieve. It's about who is smiling beside you when you get there.

SoulSync Reminder: Ambition doesn't divide love. Silence does. Speak. Support. Sync. *That is soulful success.*

CHAPTER 12

THE FINANCE & FREEDOM BALANCE, MONEY, TRUST & PARTNERSHIP IN MARRIAGE

"Money is a terrible master but an excellent servant."

– P.T. Barnum

In the sacred circle of marriage, love is the heart, but money often becomes the pulse. While emotions may unite two souls, it's the day-to-day decisions, who pays the bills, who earns more, who controls the budget, that reveal the unspoken power dynamics and emotional wounds.

Money can't replace relationships, but it can break them or build them. And in the quiet halls of countless Indian homes, it has done both. It's not the lack of love but the lack of *financial alignment* that has silently shattered many marriages. Heated arguments about spending, hidden loans, unspoken expectations, or financial dependency often begin as disagreements but deepen into emotional disconnection.

In Indian culture, where money is tied not just to needs but to identity, pride, family obligations, and social image, its role in marriage is even more complex. A rupee is never just a rupee; it carries the weight of generations, dreams, duties, and sometimes, shame.

Whether it's the husband who feels burdened as the sole earner, the wife who is questioned for wanting financial independence, or the couple navigating in-laws' expectations, money often becomes the language of love, or the lack of it.

Couples argue over spending, saving, and earning, *but the real fight is often about feeling unseen, unsafe, or unequal- like.*

"He spends on everyone except me." → translates to: *"Am I not important to him?*

"She hides purchases." → translates to: *"Will I be judged or controlled?"*

In this chapter, we gently unravel the emotional threads money weaves into marriage and learn how to transform financial friction into financial partnership, where *trust is the true currency* and *freedom is mutual.*

Case Study: The Silent Saver vs. the Spontaneous Spender

Aishwarya and Kunal, married for 8 years, are both earning professionals

- Kunal is cautious, tracks every rupee, and feels anxious without savings.
- Aishwarya believes in living life fully, weekend getaways, dining out, and gifting.

The friction? Kunal feels Aishwarya is reckless. Aishwarya feels Kunal is tight-fisted. But in deeper sessions, we discovered:

✓ Kunal's childhood was financially unstable.
✓ Aishwarya grew up in an emotionally cold home; gifts and experiences were her way of feeling alive.

Through Emotional Intelligence Coaching, they:

- Built a shared *Financial Vision Board.*
- Introduced *Joint Weekly Budgeting Ritual.*
- Created *Freedom Funds* (each gets a no-questions-asked monthly budget).

- Practiced *Empathetic Listening Exercises* about financial fears.

The result? Less blame. More understanding. And aligned spending.

Core Financial Conflicts in Marriage

✓ *Earning Imbalance:* When one earns significantly more, it may create silent power struggles or guilt.
✓ *Spending Styles:* Saver vs. spender, future-focused vs. present-joyful.
✓ *Hidden Debts / Financial Secrets:* Financial infidelity, credit card debts, secret loans, or hidden expenses.
✓ *Family Financial Obligations:* In-laws, siblings, and parental expectations can drain finances or create stress.
✓ *Delayed Joint Planning:* Avoiding discussions on kids' education, retirement, investment, or wills.

Money triggers feelings across the **shame** → **fear** → **pride** → **trust** → **joy** spectrum.

Recognize where you sit emotionally before talking about finances.

Masculine Identity & Money

Many men equate *self-worth with earning capacity.* When financial setbacks hit (layoffs, business loss), they may shut down emotionally, distancing themselves from intimacy or partnership.

SoulSync coaching helps men to separate *financial value from personal worth.*

Case Study: The Power, the Purse, and the Price of Silence, Neha & Arvind's Invisible War

> *"Money can't replace relationships, but it can break them or build them."*
>
> – **Ganesh Mandadi**

Neha and Arvind, a couple from Mumbai, looked perfect from the outside. He ran a successful logistics firm. She was a trained interior designer who took a break post-motherhood. Finances weren't a visible issue. The EMIs were managed. Vacations happened. The bills were paid.

But Neha felt like a dependent, not a partner.

She once said in session, "Even if I want to buy a Kurti, I have to wait till his mood is okay. I don't even know how much we have."

Arvind, on the other hand, believed he was being a responsible provider. "She doesn't have to worry about anything. Isn't that enough?"

Through deeper exploration, the roots emerged:

- Arvind had grown up seeing his father control every rupee and equated financial control with love and responsibility.
- Neha's parents had a hidden financial crisis that shattered her trust in not being involved.

They weren't fighting over money. They were fighting to be understood.

The healing began when they:

- Did a '*Money Story Exchange*,' where each wrote a letter to money and read it aloud.
- Introduced a '*Monthly Financial Review Ritual*' where they both saw and discussed accounts.
- Created Personal '*Freedom Funds*': no questions asked, amounts to use freely.
- Began a '*Shared Financial Goal*', saving for their daughter's design school dream.

A year later, Neha felt empowered. Arvind felt supported. And their daughter once said, "I want to be like you both, a team."

Because in marriage, financial intimacy is as vital as physical and emotional intimacy.

The Indian Financial Landscape in Marriages

Indian marriages come with unique pressures:

- Family obligations (loans for siblings, elder care)
- Guilt-laden spending (especially by women who left careers)
- Financial secrecy seen as "protective"
- Gendered money roles ("He earns, she manages" or vice versa)

But today's couples want more. They want equality in love, transparency in trust, and dignity in decisions.

Case Study: The Debt, the Dowry, and the Deep Wound, Rajesh & Keerthi's Path to Partnership

> *"A lie in a relationship needs a hundred more to survive. But the truth needs no defense—just a moment of courage."*
>
> – **SoulSync Relationships**

Rajesh and Keerthi's marriage had started with celebration and struggle. A grand wedding in Chennai, partially funded by Keerthi's family, came with unspoken expectations. Rajesh was dealing with a business loss he hadn't disclosed before marriage. Keerthi only found out six months in, when loan agents began calling.

She felt betrayed. "I thought we were building a life. Turns out, I was patching one."

Rajesh wasn't a bad man. But his shame silenced him. He thought, "Once I recover, I'll tell her. Why make her worry now?"

The breakdown came when Keerthi found out he had pawned some of the gold her parents had gifted her.

Therapy was not easy. Trust had cracked deeply. But through months of effort:

- Rajesh wrote a Financial Transparency Letter, confessing everything.
- Keerthi, though hurt, chose a path of structured forgiveness.
- They co-created a "*Financial Recovery Roadmap*" with dates, debt plans, and emotional check-ins.
- Practiced a weekly "*No Secrets Sunday*" to discuss not just money, but anything difficult.

They also redefined wealth for themselves. Not just bank balance, but truth, safety, and partnership.

Two years later, they were out of debt. But more importantly, they were rich in trust.

Coaching Tools for Financial Harmony

Tool 1: "Money & Meaning" Dialogue Date

Sit together and explore:

- What did money mean in your childhood?
- What are your top 3 money fears?
- How do you feel when your partner spends or saves?

Tool 2: Joint Budgeting Canvas

Use a visual template to map:

- Needs
- Wants
- Dreams
- Emergency buffer
- Personal fun fund

Tool 3: Financial Vision Meditation

A short guided session where couples close their eyes, breathe deeply, and *visualize their dream financial future*: the home, travels, philanthropy, security… together.

Tool 4: The "No Blame Budgeting Hour"

Weekly 30-minute session where:

- No judging each other's purchases
- Discuss only *what's working*
- End with gratitude for each other's efforts

Because shared money doesn't mean shared power. Shared understanding does.

Spiritual Insight: Lakshmi, Not Just Wealth, But Presence

In Indian traditions, Goddess Lakshmi represents not just material wealth, but grace, beauty, abundance, and alignment. She enters where there is harmony, honesty, and invitation.

True wealth in a marriage is when money flows through love, not over silence.

As a Vedic verse says:

"Where the woman is respected and heard, there resides prosperity."

SoulSync Practice: *The Money Mirror*

In every couple's journey, there comes a moment where money becomes more than numbers; it becomes a mirror. It reflects our upbringing, reveals our fears, and sometimes, distorts our perception of each other. When financial arguments arise, they often stem not from the lack of funds, but from the lack of shared emotional language around money.

Before any practical budgeting tool or investment plan can work, we must begin with *emotional clarity*. And that begins with introspection.

This guided reflection is designed to bring hidden beliefs, childhood patterns, and unmet emotional needs to the surface, so they can be healed and harmonized together.

Take a quiet hour alone or with your partner. Light a candle. Pour some chai. And gently explore:

The Money Values Map

1. *What emotions do I associate with money?*
   Is it safety? Pride? Control? Fear? Guilt? Abundance? Reflect on how you *feel* when money enters or exits your life.
2. *Which childhood memory shaped my beliefs about money the most?*
   Was it a time of lack, excess, debt, generosity, or secrecy? What did your parents fight or worry about when it came to money?
3. *What does "financial freedom" mean to me personally, and emotionally?*
   Is it about owning a home? Having choices? Being debt-free? Supporting parents? Funding dreams? There's no wrong answer, only honest ones.
4. *How can we honor both our money styles, without blame or dominance?*

Is one a saver and the other a spender? One a risk-taker and the other a security-seeker? Instead of changing each other, how can you *complement* each other?

When partners learn each other's financial DNA, judgment dissolves. And in its place arises empathy and collaboration.

SoulSync Reminder: A rich marriage is one where conversations flow freely, not just currency.

Final SoulSync Reflection on Wealth and Love

- *Money isn't the enemy; emotional misunderstanding is.*

A rupee is neutral. It's what we project onto it, fear, pride, guilt, or security, that makes it heavy or healing.

- *Finance conversations need empathy, not ego.*

It's not about who earns more, who saves better, or who spends less. It's about *transparency,* *respect,* and shared goals that nourish both souls.

- *The wealthiest couples aren't those with the biggest bank accounts, but those with the deepest trust.*

Trust, when combined with clarity and mutual vision, becomes the true currency of a resilient relationship. Because real wealth is not what you earn. It's who you can count on when it matters most.

As you walk this sacred path together, may your love be the vault, your trust the interest, and your shared dreams the priceless treasure.

CHAPTER 13

PURPOSEFUL PARTNERSHIP, DESIGNING A MARRIAGE THAT SERVES THE WORLD

"The meeting of two personalities is like the contact of two chemical substances: if there is any reaction, both are transformed."

– **Carl Gustav Jung**

There comes a stage in many enduring marriages when the silence between conversations begins to whisper something deeper, a calling that stretches beyond shared calendars and daily comfort. It's a subtle shift from asking, *"What are we building for ourselves?"* to wondering, *"What are we building beyond ourselves?"*

This is the moment when love matures into contribution. When couples realize that fulfillment isn't only about emotional intimacy or material stability, but about shared purpose. In Indian marriages, where family, dharma, and legacy often intertwine, this question holds even more weight. What if our partnership was not just to support each other, but to uplift the world?

Welcome to the sacred evolution of *Purposeful Partnership.*

The SoulSync Hierarchy of Couple Needs

From Survival to Sacred Service, "The Maslowian Journey of Modern Love"

"When two people connect deeply, they don't just fulfill each other, they elevate the world."

Maslow's classic pyramid of human needs becomes even more powerful when viewed through the lens of a committed relationship. When two individuals journey through these layers *together*, the relationship becomes not just a partnership, but a spiritual path.

Let's explore each level in the context of *Indian couple dynamics*, from *basic bonding* to *conscious contribution.*

1. Physical & Physiological Safety: "We're Safe Together"

This is the foundation. In this stage, couples focus on:

- Food, shelter, health, and routine.
- Shared physical environment: safe home, steady income, secure lifestyle.

In Indian marriages, this often includes joint family security, navigating in-law expectations, and financial grounding.

Manifestation: Trust builds when couples feel protected, fed, and physically secure together.

Climb Signal: Once survival is stable, the heart yearns for connection, not just comfort.

2. *Emotional & Psychological Safety: "I Can Be Me with You"*

Here, couples need:

- Open communication without fear of judgment.
- Safe emotional expression, anger, grief, desire, dreams.
- Validation and presence.

Especially in arranged setups, this stage is the turning point, from "playing roles" to "revealing souls."

Manifestation: Fights reduce. Vulnerability increases. Silence becomes soft, not sharp.

Climb Signal: When partners stop hiding their truth, they begin seeking deeper intimacy.

3. Love & Belonging: "We Choose Each Other, Daily"

Now the bond deepens:

- Feeling wanted, desired, seen.
- Shared rituals, a couple times, affectionate language.
- Emotional rituals like "thank you circles" or nightly check-ins.

In Indian marriages, this often includes creating couple-space in joint-family systems, making each other a priority amidst collective expectations.

Manifestation: They speak a shared emotional language. They say "we" more than "I".

Climb Signal: With love anchored, the need to grow as individuals (yet together) arises.

4. Esteem & Growth: "I'm Growing, You're Growing, We're Growing"

Here, the focus shifts to:

- Mutual respect for ambitions, dreams, passions.
- Encouragement, not competition.
- Celebrating each other's wins.

When one partner grows while the other stays stagnant, friction brews. True esteem means both partners flourish.

Manifestation:

Partners feel inspired, not insecure, around each other.

Climb Signal: With individual esteem secure, couples start asking, *"What can we create together?"*

5. *Shared Purpose & Contribution: "Our Love is Our Legacy"*

This is the summit of couple hood. The purpose stage. Together, couples now:

- Serve a cause beyond themselves.
- Mentor others, volunteer, raise conscious children, or build impact-led initiatives.
- Let their love ripple into the world.

This is the Grihastha ideal, not just raising a home, but raising consciousness through that home.

Manifestation: Love becomes prayer. Service becomes joy. Marriage becomes a mission.

Ultimate Arrival: They no longer ask "What do I get?" They now ask, "What do we give?"

The Pyramid in Practice: A Summary Reflection

Level	Need	SoulSync Activation
1. *Physical Safety*	Security, shelter, food	Build a grounded lifestyle and home.

2. *Emotional Safety*	Trust, vulnerability, acceptance	Create space for honest, judgment-free expression.
3. *Love & Belonging*	Affection, connection, presence	Rituals of togetherness and prioritizing each other.
4. *Esteem & Growth*	Achievement, validation, purpose	Celebrate each other's individuality.
5. *Purpose & Legacy*	Contribution, meaning, impact	Serve the world together from your shared soul.

"Strong relationships aren't born — they're built with trust, effort, and emotional presence."

– **SoulSync Relationships**

SoulSync Insight

"A relationship is not just a place to love. It's a place to evolve. To heal. To grow. And finally, to give."

True fulfillment in marriage is not just when partners meet *each other's* needs…

It's when their love begins to meet the world's.

Let your pyramid of love rise, not as a monument of comfort, but as a temple of meaning.

Case Study: Sahana & Dev, From Power Couple to Purpose Couple

> *"Marriage isn't about staying in love; it's about growing in love, together."*
>
> **– SoulSync Relationships**

Sahana and Dev were once the textbook definition of success: top-tier corporate jobs, high-rise living, exotic vacations, and a tightly planned family calendar. But in their quiet moments, they often felt... empty.

Then came a wake-up call, a health crisis in their family. It shook their well-structured lives, and for the first time, they paused.

They began volunteering on weekends, mentoring young students from underserved communities. "It wasn't just about healing others," Dev said. "It healed something within *us*."

That experience marked the beginning of their purpose journey. Today, they co-run a values-based education startup and hold monthly couple-visioning sessions to keep their mission aligned.

Their relationship transformed from a successful unit to a significant force.

Are You and Your Partner Ready for a Purposeful Shift?

Here are signs a couple is evolving toward purpose:

- You've reached material milestones, but feel emotionally or spiritually undernourished.
- There's a yearning for "more," without knowing exactly what that is.
- Conflicts now arise more around *meaning* than tasks, questions like "Why are we doing this?"
- A shared event (illness, loss, a spiritual experience) shifts your priorities.
- Children are becoming independent, and suddenly, there's space and silence.

These aren't signs of decline. They're signs of awakening.

SoulSync Practice: Emotional Intelligence Meets Purpose Activation

At SoulSync, we believe that emotional safety is the seedbed of soul purpose. Once couples stabilize their emotional ground, they are uniquely poised to create something beautiful together, beyond themselves.

Here are the tools we share with couples on this sacred journey:

Tool 1: Couple Visioning Canvas

Take out a blank journal page and divide it into four quadrants:

1. *Our Shared Values* – What matters to us most deeply?
2. *Who We Love to Help* – Children? Women? Nature? The elderly?
3. *What We're Passionate About* – What excites us or makes us come alive?
4. *What the World Needs* – What breaks our heart or ignites our compassion?

At the *intersection* of all four lies your *Couple Ikigai*, your shared soul purpose.

"We realized we both love storytelling and children. We now host storytelling Saturdays in orphanages."

Tool 2: Purpose Check-In Questions

Use these to open soulful dialogues:

- What would we regret not doing together in this lifetime?
- If our relationship could *heal* something in the world, what would that be?
- Where do we lose track of time when we're together?

- Whose life would change if we simply showed up as a team?

Make this a monthly ritual. Brew some tea. Light a candle. Listen deeply.

The 3 Circles of a Purposeful Marriage

Imagine your relationship as a ripple with three powerful layers:

1. *[ME]*, Your self-realization and authenticity
2. *[WE]*, The emotional and intimate partnership you share
3. *[BEYOND]*, The impact you make as a couple on the world

A Purposeful Partnership dances between all three. The beauty lies in the balance.

Case Study: From Accidental Healers to Intentional Helpers, Leela & Raghav

Leela and Raghav, both medical professionals in Hyderabad, had spent a decade climbing the ladders of success. They had two children, a comfortable home, and enviable positions in their respective hospitals. But an encounter during a family vacation to a tribal region changed everything.

They met a local midwife, 72 years old, who had been delivering babies without formal training or tools. Her wisdom amazed them, but so did the poverty around her. The disparity haunted them long after they returned home.

"We realized," said Leela, "that our skills were trapped in city hospitals while lives were waiting to be touched elsewhere."

Instead of quitting their jobs, they began small: a weekend health camp, monthly rural visits, and sourcing equipment donations. Over time, this turned into a registered initiative training local healthcare workers in basic maternal and child care.

Their marriage changed, too. Arguments about fatigue and parenting gaps gave way to shared planning, meaningful late-night talks, and purpose-driven parenting.

Key Practices Applied:

- Created a *Couple Purpose Journal* to document ideas, emotions, and mission goals.
- Began *Value Alignment Circles* every fortnight to check if their work aligned with their family values.
- Practiced *SoulSync Breathing Rituals* before community visits to ground their intentions.

Their children often joined the camps. And the joy on their faces wasn't just pride in their parents, it was the birth of empathy. Leela and Raghav became more than healers. They became torchbearers of compassionate partnership.

The Anatomy of a Purposeful Partnership

Purposeful marriages don't begin with a grand vision, or don't have to mean starting an NGO. They begin with a question: *What do we have, together, that the world needs?*

When couples stop seeing their relationship as the destination and start seeing it as a vehicle, the journey transforms.

In Indian tradition, the *Grihastha* life stage is not just about raising a family; it's about contributing to society through that family. It's about a spiritual partnership in daily life.

Purpose may look like:

- Mentoring newly married couples or teenagers
- Adopting eco-conscious habits for sustainable living
- Volunteering at a school
- Starting a mindful parenting blog
- Write, speak, or create content that inspires
- Supporting a cause close to your shared heart

Remember: It's not about how *big* your contribution is. It's about how *true* and *shared* it is.

Case Study: From Fracture to Foundation, The Renewal of Sanjay & Meera

Sanjay and Meera were on the verge of separation when they arrived for coaching. Sanjay, a successful builder in Delhi, was driven, ambitious, and emotionally distant. Meera, a former school teacher, had quit her job to raise their two children and now felt invisible.

The fracture ran deep. Years of unspoken resentment, unequal power dynamics, and emotional abandonment had pushed them to the edge. Meera often said, "I'm a ghost in my own home."

But one night, after a particularly emotional session, they both sat under the stars outside the coaching center.

"Why are we still here?" Sanjay asked.

"Because I still want this to mean something," Meera replied.

That was the beginning. Not of romantic reconciliation, but of mutual rebirth.

Together, they revisited an old dream, opening a learning space for underprivileged kids in Sanjay's construction sites. Meera took the lead. Sanjay offered his buildings for after-school use. Slowly, they began to reconnect, not through affection first, but through *shared service*.

It wasn't easy. There were setbacks, tears, and days of disconnection. But they stuck to:

- The *Purpose Check-In Ritual* every Sunday, asking, "What did we do this week that mattered to someone else?"
- Practicing *Appreciative Dialogue* rather than conflict-replay.
- Writing a *Couple Mission Scroll,* which now hangs in their children's room.

Six years later, that space has evolved into a full-fledged learning center. Sanjay and Meera still argue, but now, they argue in the direction of growth, not retreat.

Their truth: Sometimes, the way back to love is not inward, but outward.

Reflection Journal for Couples

Use these prompts to explore your shared path:

- What values do we never want to compromise on?
- What breaks our heart so deeply, we're moved to act?
- If we had just one year left together, what would we do?
- Who in our community needs what we already have?

Key Takeaways

A *Purposeful Marriage* aligns passion, compassion, and action.

- It turns private love into public good.
- It awakens a deeper bond through shared giving and soulful service.
- It moves a couple from "me and you" to "we, for the world."

Spiritual Insight: *Dharma Beyond the Doorstep*

Indian scriptures often remind us: *Seva* (selfless service) is not a separate act from family life. It's embedded within it.

When couples serve together, their relationship becomes a temple, where love is the deity and contribution is the daily offering.

SoulSync Affirmation: *"We are not just partners in love. We are co-creators of meaning. Together, our hearts serve, and our love flows outward."*

Final Reflection: What Will Be Your Legacy of Love?

When the noise of the world fades and the years have passed, what will remain?

The vacations will blur. The gifts will age. But the kindness you created as a couple, the lives you touched, the children you mentored, the earth you respected, will echo on and live forever in its legacy.

That is the essence of *Purposeful Partnership*.

CHAPTER 14

THE RITUAL OF RENEWAL, SUSTAINING LOVE WITH SACRED PRACTICE

"A thriving relationship is like a garden, it won't bloom forever without pruning, watering, and daily light from your presence."

– **Ganesh Mandadi**

Even the most exquisite garden, left unattended, will wither. Even the fittest athlete, without consistent practice, will lose their form. And even the deepest, most soulful love will eventually fade, if not nurtured.

Relationships are not one-time victories. They are not static accomplishments. They are living, breathing ecosystems that need tending, pruning, and replenishing.

Just as a world-class athlete trains every day, not because they've forgotten how to play, but because they know mastery is sustained, not inherited, so must couples invest in their bond.

No matter how strong your connection is today, it will not sustain itself tomorrow without intention.

Most relationships don't break apart because of one grand failure. They quietly wither from absence, of presence, of intention, of meaning.

In the everyday rhythm of life, the rushed mornings, the distracted dinners, the emotional silences, love gets quietly buried under routine. What starts as a soul-deep connection often fades into a survival partnership. But it doesn't have to.

What if your relationship had sacred pauses? What if love were renewed like seasons, not once in a while, but every day, every week, every year?

This chapter is not about fixing what's broken or adding more to your already full plate. It's about preventing the erosion of what's beautiful. It's a gentle reminder that love, to stay alive, must be renewed, consistently, consciously, and sacredly.

Why Renewal Matters More Than Romance

> *"Rock bottom is a place where ego dies and authenticity is born."*
>
> – **Ganesh Mandadi**

Marriages often start with a spark but thrive with steady light. In the rush of life, we forget that even love needs daily oxygen. Over time, what once felt vibrant becomes routine. The passion that once flowed effortlessly now needs direction.

But the solution isn't grand gestures. It's in the quiet discipline of care.

Like a gardener waters every morning or an artist sketches daily, couples must craft sacred spaces to reconnect, before disconnection becomes the default.

Rituals are not routines; they are reminders. Reminders that even in chaos, there is us. Even in fatigue, there is room for affection. Even in silence, there is presence.

Case Study: The Athlete's Marriage, Reclaiming Intimacy Through Intentional Practice

Naveen, a former state-level sprinter, and Ananya, a Kathak dancer turned school teacher, had been married for 11 years. They understood discipline. They understood the power of practice.

Yet, somewhere between work, parenting, and daily demands, they had stopped practicing *each other*.

"Every day, I warm up before my runs," Naveen once said. "But I didn't warm up before conversations with her."

Their marriage hadn't cracked, but it had calcified. Laughter became rare. Touch became absent. Conversations were transactional.

In their SoulSync sessions, we invited them to view their relationship like their art, something that needed rhythm, effort, and renewal.

They began small:

- A morning hand-hold while sipping chai on the balcony.
- Midweek surprise texts recalling their early courtship.
- A Sunday ritual called "Stretch & Share," where they did simple yoga stretches while speaking about one emotional high and one low from the week.

Ananya said, "We stopped trying to impress each other. And started impressing intention into our love."

After 90 days of consistent ritual practice, they reported a sense of *newness*, like they were learning each other all over again. Their children noticed it too. One of them even said, "You both laugh more now."

Sometimes, renewal is not about reinventing love. It's about remembering it, daily.

> *"You don't need perfect people in your relationships — you need emotionally honest and balanced ones."*
>
> – **SoulSync Relationships**

Ancient Wisdom: Time as a Sacred Offering

In ancient Indian traditions, rituals weren't grand or exclusive. They were subtle, rhythmic acts that made everyday life sacred.

- "*Samskāras*" marked transitions, from birth to union, from dusk to dawn.
- "*Shraddha*" meant heartfelt devotion, not just doing things, but *offering* yourself to them.
- Cooking was worship. Silence was a prayer.
- And relationships? They were seen as a spiritual path.
  - A glance offered with presence.
  - A touch given with love.
  - A word spoken with awareness.

These were the sacred fires couples lit every day.

Let's bring that wisdom back into the now.

Case Study: When the Flame Flickered, Rebuilding After the Break

> *"A great marriage is not when the perfect couple comes together. It is when an imperfect couple learns to enjoy their differences."*
>
> – **Dave Meurer**

For Manish and Trisha, the word "renewal" felt too late. After 14 years of marriage, emotional betrayal had left their bond in tatters. Manish had developed a deep emotional connection with a colleague, and though it never became physical, it broke Trisha's trust.

She said, "He didn't cheat with his body. But he cheated with his presence."

Manish was remorseful. He hadn't meant for it to happen; it was just that Trisha and he had stopped *being us*. She became the home manager; he became the provider. But they no longer saw each other.

In one of our SoulSync Healing Circles, the couple was asked: "What would you do differently if today were Day 1 of your marriage?"

Trisha whispered, "I'd make us a daily ritual, not a monthly reminder."

They began with silence, not words. Ten minutes every evening sitting beside each other, holding hands, breathing together.

Then came ritual repair:

- Weekly written letters exchanged, even when angry.
- A Renewal Vow every month, one line: "This month, I promise to…"
- A Healing Journal, where they noted every moment that felt emotionally safe.

It wasn't easy. There were relapses. But renewal isn't perfection, it's persistence.

Two years later, they renew their vows annually with close friends. Their marriage didn't just survive. It re-bloomed.

Lesson? Renewal is not a miracle. It's a mindset.

Everyday Renewal: The Sacred Maintenance Plan

Think of your relationship like a sacred garden. What does it need?

- *Sunlight of presence:* Time without distractions.
- *Water of words:* Daily affirmations, gratitude, check-ins.
- *Fertilizer of fun:* Laughter, play, spontaneity.
- *Pruning of pain:* Honest conversations about what's not working.

Just as no athlete reaches excellence without daily effort, no marriage sustains joy without consistent nurturing.

SoulSync Tip: Use your toothbrush time or chai moments as emotional check-ins instead of scrolling time.

SoulSync Ritual: The Renewal Tracker

Create a monthly calendar where you track:

- One Daily Connection Moment
- One Weekly Shared Experience
- One Monthly Reflection Evening

Stick it on your fridge or your bedside. Watch love become a habit.

Wisdom from Indian Traditions: Samskara of Sustenance
In ancient Indian culture, *samskaras* weren't just rites of passage; they were reminders to pause, reflect, and renew. Every major life event was honored not once but annually.

Marriage anniversaries weren't celebrations of endurance; they were calls for recommitment.

Let your rituals echo that legacy. Light a diya together. Whisper a prayer. Prepare a simple thali of gratitude. Remind each other: *We choose this love again, today.*

SoulSync Affirmations

- "Our love grows not by chance, but by choice, every day."

- "We don't wait for magic, we create it, again and again."
- "Ritual is the soil where our forever takes root."

Final Reflection: Are You Training Your Love?

The best athletes train daily. The most admired artists practice even after mastery. Not because they need to, but because they know excellence demands renewal.

Why should love be any different?

Your relationship is not just a feeling. It's a form. A practice. A sacred performance of presence.

So ask yourself:

- Are we nourishing or neglecting our bond?
- Are we rehearsing resentment or reactivating renewal?
- Are we showing up tired, or tuned in?

You don't need more time. You need more *intention.* And the courage to keep beginning again.

Because great love doesn't just happen.

It's trained.

It's nurtured.

It's renewed.

Every single day.

CONCLUSION: FROM CONFLICT TO CONNECTION, FROM LOVE TO LEGACY

> *"Love is a place. When you go there, you'll see everything differently."*
>
> – **Rumi**

Every relationship begins with a spark, sometimes bright, sometimes gentle. But the journey that follows is never a straight line. It's a spiral of discovery, healing, and rediscovery. And as you arrive at the final page of *Modern Couples, Ancient Wisdom*, pause, not to end this journey, but to lean into a sacred beginning.

This book was not meant to teach you how to "manage" your marriage. That's too small a word for something as immense as love. It was created as an invitation to awaken, to turn your relationship into a soulful living space where ancient truths meet modern lives, and where conflict becomes the compost for blooming connection.

If there's one truth that echoes through every page, it is this: *Nothing sustains itself without tending. Not even love.*

Just as the strongest athlete trains daily to remain agile and resilient, and just as a lush garden stays alive only through persistent care, relationships too require nourishment, presence, effort, and renewal.

Even the best match loses its fire if left unattended. Even the wisest partners forget without reminders. What saves us is not intensity, but intimacy. Not perfection, but presence.

We walked through seasons together, chapters of inner discovery and relational growth, not as lessons but as lanterns.

You've uncovered the emotional DNA that shapes how you show up.

You've seen how childhood wounds ripple into adult intimacy and how healing is not only personal but relational.

You've faced the tremors of betrayal and mistrust, and found that even the most broken moments can become bridges, if crossed with courage.

You've explored how shared dreams, conscious parenting, and spiritual alignment can transform routine marriage into a soulful union.

You've learned the sacred art of rituals, not as tasks, but as tender threads that keep love visible and vibrant.

Most importantly, you've begun to remember something our ancestors always knew,

That marriage is not just about companionship. It is about *conscious co-creation.* It is the soil where you grow not just together, but beyond yourselves.

And now, as you close this chapter, not just of a book, but perhaps of a certain phase in your love, ask yourself gently:

What is the legacy of our love?

Who will be transformed by our togetherness?

What part of us will still shine... even when we're gone?

You don't need to have all the answers. But you must keep asking.

Let your life become the embodiment of the truths you've remembered here. Let your relationship be the sanctuary where these truths breathe.

Revisit. Rebuild. Renew.

Not because love is lost. But because love is living.

And anything alive must be nourished again and again.

So start small.

Whisper instead of reacting.

Sit closer than usual.

Light a lamp for no reason.

Make eye contact long enough to see the soul beneath the face.

Say, "I choose you," not because it's Valentine's Day, but because it's *today*.

And if you ever forget, return to these pages. They are not ink on paper. They are footprints in sand, leading you home.

Your marriage isn't a destination. It is a dharma.

A sacred path to walk, imperfectly, honestly, lovingly.

As we part from this written journey, remember:

You carry not just insights, but invitations.
Not just tools, but truths.
Not just knowledge, but the courage to love deeply and consciously.

With reverence for your path and belief in your love,
May you walk forward not just as a modern couple,

But as timeless partners, shaping a soulful legacy.

– ***Ganesh Mandadi***

Gratitude Note from Author

Dear Reader,

From the stillness of my heart to the quiet corners of yours, thank you.

Thank you not just for reading these pages, but for meeting them with openness, courage, and a willingness to reflect. In a world that often seeks speed over depth, you chose presence. That alone makes you part of a quiet revolution, one that believes love is worth the work.

This book was born not in theory, but in the fire of lived experience, as a husband who has stumbled, softened, and stayed; as a coach who has witnessed couples lean in when leaving seemed easier; and as a lifelong seeker of what it truly means to love with soul.

I've come to believe that relationships are not problems to solve, but sacred paths to walk. They are invitations to heal what's unspoken, to grow into what's possible, and to remember who we are at our most human and most divine.

If even one sentence in this book helped you pause with compassion or hold your partner with more presence, then its purpose has been served.

My hope is not just that you stay together,

But that you awaken together.

That your love becomes not a story of survival, but of soulful flourishing.

May your partnership be your prayer.
May your healing be your offering.
And may your journey forward be guided by grace.

With deep gratitude,
Ganesh Mandadi
Founder, *SoulSync Relationships*™
Relationship & Life Balance Coach | Author | Speaker

Bonus Resource Page

30 Ritual Prompts for Sacred Connection

Simple, soulful practices to renew your bond, one sacred moment at a time.

In the chaos of everyday life, we often forget that connection doesn't require grand gestures, it simply needs presence, intention, and sacred pauses. These 30 ritual prompts are designed to help couples bring emotional intimacy, soulful bonding, and spiritual presence into their relationship rhythm.

Categorized into *Daily*, *Weekly*, and *Monthly/Seasonal* practices, they offer gentle yet powerful ways to sync with each other's hearts. You don't have to perform every ritual - *even adopting one or two from each category can bring immense transformation and emotional nourishment*. It's not about doing more, but about doing it meaningfully.

Let your rituals be soft anchors—not obligations, but offerings of love.

Daily Ritual Prompts (Infuse each day with mindful love & soulful presence)

Start and end your day with micro-moments that turn routine into ritual.

1. *3-Minute Morning Eye Gaze*

Sit in silence facing each other. Let your eyes be the window to your souls, saying what words cannot.

2. *Touch Ritual Before Leaving*
   Whether it's a forehead kiss, lingering hug, or a hand over the heart, let each parting be a sacred moment.
3. *Shared Breath Meditation*
   Before sleep, sit or lie down and breathe in sync for 2 minutes. Feel each other's calm, tension, or energy without needing words.
4. *Gratitude Exchange at Dinner*
   Over your evening meal, share one specific thing you appreciated about each other that day.
5. *Mini Love Note or Post-It Surprise*
   Hide a loving note in unexpected places, wallets, books, lunch boxes, with a memory, affirmation, or compliment.
6. *Water Blessing Together*
   Hold hands, offer a silent or whispered thank-you to nature and each other before sipping your first glass of water.
7. *"Body, Mind, Heart" Check-in*
   Ask: "How's your body today? Your mind? Your heart?" and just listen, without fixing.
8. *Evening Aromatherapy Wind-Down*
   Choose calming oils or incense, light them together, and take a few minutes to reflect on the highs and lows of the day.

9. *Daily Touchpoint Timer*
   Set a recurring timer as a loving nudge to send a 2-minute appreciation or check-in message during the workday.
10. *Mirror Affirmations Together*
    Stand side by side and reflect on one thing you admire in each other and yourself. Let your reflection become a reminder of love.

Weekly Ritual Prompts *(Reset your connection through rhythm & emotional depth)*

These practices help couples slow down, tune in, and recharge emotionally.

1. *Sunday "Heart Talk Hour"*
   Create a no-distractions space for one hour to share openly, highs, lows, dreams, fears, and silent hopes.
2. *Intimacy Reconnection Night*
   Let go of performance. Explore closeness through cuddles, touch, sensuality, or deep laughter, follow the heart, not habit.
3. *"Switch Roles" Fun Day*
   Step into each other's shoes for a day. Cook, clean, or take over responsibilities to break patterns and deepen empathy.

4. *Love Jar Sharing*
   Keep a jar filled with loving notes or shared memories. Each week, pick one and relive the moment together.
5. *Joint Journaling Time*
   Spend 15 quiet minutes writing about your feelings, then read aloud to each other. Vulnerability becomes a bridge.
6. *Cook One Meal Together*
   Choose a nostalgic or culturally meaningful recipe. Cook with teamwork and serve it with stories.
7. *Spiritual Time Together*
   Sit for a short meditation, chant, prayer, or read from a spiritual book. Connect through silence and soul.
8. *Dance in the Living Room*
   Play a favorite song from your early days and dance like you're 20 again. Let your hearts move, not just your feet.
9. *Silent Walk in Nature*
   Take a walk together without talking. Notice your breath, the trees, the wind, and each other's quiet companionship.
10. *Forgiveness & Appreciation Circle*
    Take turns sharing one hurt and one appreciation. Listen without defending. Hold space. Then switch roles.

Monthly & Seasonal Ritual Prompts *(Celebrate growth, mark cycles & honor your sacred journey together)*

These rituals invite intentional reflection, soulful release, and shared renewal.

1. *New Moon Intentions Together*
   On every new moon, write down one intention as a couple. Place it near your bed or altar. Let it guide your month.
2. *Full Moon Release Ritual*
   Write down what you're ready to release, from old resentments to limiting patterns. Burn the note and embrace afterward.
3. *Quarterly Relationship Check-In*
   Reflect on what's thriving, what's challenging, and what you want to build. Use it to realign your vision.
4. *Seasonal Couple Cleanse*
   Choose a detox for mind, body, or space, a tech-free weekend, a healthy food cleanse, or digital minimalism.
5. *Create a Couple Vision Board*
   Cut, draw, or digitally design your shared goals, travel, family, lifestyle, or purpose, and place it somewhere visible.
6. *Anniversary of First Meeting Ritual*
   Revisit the place or memory of your first meeting. Recreate the joy, the butterflies, and the innocence.

7. *Relationship Book Night*
   Choose a chapter from a relationship-enhancing book. Read it aloud and discuss insights over herbal tea or wine.
8. *Blessing Your Space*
   Use camphor, incense, or bells to cleanse and bless each room. Invite peace, love, and fresh energy into your home.
9. *Celebrate Small Wins Day*
   Acknowledge small victories like resolving an argument mindfully or supporting each other during a tough week.
10. *Ritual of Renewal – Vow Reaffirmation*
    Once a year or each season, write and speak updated vows. Let your evolving love be witnessed, honored, and renewed.

SoulSync Note:

These rituals aren't about perfection, they're about presence. Pick one or two from each category to begin. Let them become anchors of intimacy, trust, and renewal. Over time, these sacred practices will shape a deeper, more soulful journey of togetherness.

ABOUT THE AUTHOR - GANESH MANDADI

Certified Relationship & Life Balance Coach, Certified NLP Practitioner, MBA, CMA, PMP, OCS

Ganesh Mandadi is a TEDx and Josh Talks speaker, author of Your Life Graduation, and the visionary founder of SoulSync Relationships™. With over two decades of transformational work in life, love, and leadership, he has become a trusted voice in healing relationships and guiding professionals toward balance, harmony, and purposeful growth.

From being a school dropout to earning global credentials, Ganesh's journey is a living testament to resilience, reinvention, and purpose. His mission is to help couples and professionals transform conflict into connection, imbalance into harmony, and stress into soulful productivity through relationship coaching, learning communities, and practical tools that sustain love and growth in everyday life.

Blending ancient Indian spiritual wisdom with modern emotional intelligence, NLP techniques, and real-life marital insights, Ganesh's approach is both practical and profoundly healing. His authenticity—rooted in personal struggles, a long-term marriage, and an unwavering passion to serve—sets him apart as a relationship guide who speaks not just from theory but from lived experience.

Through retreats, coaching, and his heartfelt writings, Ganesh is working towards his vision of a world where love and life flow together — strong marriages, fulfilled individuals, and thriving communities. His book is an offering of hope and transformation, helping couples and professionals create relationships that are conscious, sacred, and enduring in today's fast-paced, digitally disruptive world.